Newlyweds Afloat

NEWLYWEDS AFLOAT

Married Bliss
and
Mechanical Breakdowns
While Living Aboard a Trawler

Felicia Schneiderhan

BREAKAWAY BOOKS
HALCOTTSVILLE, NEW YORK
2015

ISBN: 978-1-62124-020-4
Library of Congress Control Number: 2015945490

Published by Breakaway Books
P.O. Box 24
Halcottsville, NY 12438
www.breakawaybooks.com

Excerpts have previously appeared in the *Chicago Sun-Times, Lake Superior Magazine, PassageMaker Magazine, Lake Magazine,* and *Buffalo Carp.*

Acknowledgments

The author owes a boatload of gratitude to Garth Battista and Breakaway Books, Pamela Mittlefehldt, Julie Buckles, Sue Collins, Irene Blakely and Blakely's Hill House, the Arrowhead Regional Arts Council, Kathy Lesinski, Erika Mikkalo, Jenny Seay, Marcia Brenner, Mary Colleran, Chris Quillian, Carl Rabe, Anne Nordhaus-Bike, Mark Mershon, Jeff Bishop, Jeff & Gail, Patty Dillon, Sandy Lemieux, Lois Blau, Eric May, Steve & Cindy, Denise Power, Patty Young, Carol Dunbar, Catherine Meier, Jill & Scott & Sophia, John & Ed, Mom & Dad, Ed & Carol, and the beloved, raucous, ever-helpful River Rats. Much love to Rafe, Esther, and Anton. And for Mark, who had a vision and went for it— and brought me along for the ride.

FIRST EDITION

CONTENTS

For Mark

My curiosity had been aroused, that curiosity peculiar to all those who travel over the water, which makes you want to see everything, watch everything closely, which makes you passionately interested in the slightest things.

—Guy de Maupassant, *Afloat*

I DON'T USUALLY LIVE THIS WAY

The summer I was thirty years old, my husband moved out. I set up a sewing machine in the dining room of our second-floor Chicago apartment. In my underwear with hair pulled high, I toiled over a new wardrobe in a heat-wave frenzy. I drank whiskey and spewed aggression by running long seams under the needle, sweat splashing down onto short silky skirts and blouses with plunging cowl necklines. I was determined to transform myself into someone new, someone I thought I was meant to be, had I not been held back by a bad marriage and a bad job and a bad go of things.

Who I had been: a girl from the Mississippi River, the daughter of a former Catholic nun caught by a Wisconsin fisherman. Estranged from my Catholic faith and missing it. A theater undergrad, a fiction writing MFA. In a thirteen-year "open" relationship with a high school boyfriend that was more often about being roommates and drinking buddies than lovers. My soon-to-be-ex once told me, "You're not as attractive as you'd like to be, but more attractive than you think you are."

Who I thought I was meant to be: Sassy-Sex-and-the-City-Hip-Young-Creative-Urban-Single-Female. Yeah.

The truth: That summer, I was neither. I was in the crazy liminal space when life as we know it is ending and a new life—with limitless possibilities—is about to begin. It is the hazy inch between horizon and sky, where familiar objects become murky, our perception distorted by distance and the earth's curve. It can be incredibly painful, as much as inspiring and exhilarating. As my mind reeled with the potential paths for my new life (new job? move to London?), I gravitated toward the familiar: drinking and men.

Even in the "openness" my ex and I had shared, the boundaries were blurred and there was always something covert about my actions, even if I blurted them out later in guilt-fueled confessions. This new single-dom was something different; it was totally acceptable—even *encouraged*—to date as many men as I wanted.

I went on first dates with no thought of a second. Anyone was up for consideration: an architect, a reporter just back from Iraq, a temp worker who collected furniture to sell on eBay. The temp and I got along pretty well; we both liked jazz and expensive whiskey and thinking about ourselves. While I sat on one of four soon-to-be-sold couches in his living room, he looked at me over his drink and said, "I don't usually live this way." I burst out laughing. He couldn't have explained my life any better.

One Saturday afternoon I left my new wardrobe at home in favor of a T-shirt and cargo pants and headed out to the suburbs for my best friend's casual coed bridal shower.

As my marriage was ending, Jill was about to take the leap.

I felt conspicuous just driving out to the party.

The party was given by three of Jill's fellow medical residents; they had grown close over residency, and these days it seemed she had more in common with them than with me; they were all married with children and real careers. They had houses.

I wasn't sure what Jill's fiancé thought of me, either. Scott lived in Detroit, and the few times I had met him weren't my best moments. At my husband's birthday party I shook Scott's hand, dropped my second vodka martini, later passed out. I didn't think he liked the idea of me standing with them at the altar as her maid of honor, the scarlet D pasted to my chest.

But what could I do? Jill and I had been friends since seventh grade. She was in love, I was happy for her. I would try to be on my best behavior.

There wasn't a lot to be done for the party; the crudités waited on pretty platters, the grill smoldered. I made awkward small talk with doctors and lawyers and when someone asked me where my husband was, I quietly told her we were splitting up. It was so recent, hardly anyone knew about it.

It felt strange to be standing at the party without him. For so long I had felt tied into our shared identity, the way people start to look alike after decades together. We were less than a year apart in age, the same height. I could almost see him there beside me, with his mass of thick curly light-brown hair. His facial hair constantly changed, along with his physique; slimmed down during marathon training, rounded out during the off-season. We would probably be high, after smoking pot on the car ride out to the suburbs, and conversation with professionals would be strained. I would be impatient and daydreaming, just as I was without him.

As I stood in the dining room, looking out through the sliding glass doors to the tiny suburban backyard, there suddenly appeared a man barreling up, heading straight for us. He was short, compact, with a Buddha belly beneath a blue Hawaiian shirt. His hair was salt and pepper around the edges. He moved fast, propelled by burly arms, intent. *He must know somebody,* I thought, *to be so confident and comfortable walking in through the back door.*

The groom appeared at my side. "Here comes Mark," he said,

going out to greet his brother with a huge hug.

Though I didn't recall it then, I had met Mark two years earlier when he and Scott came to move Jill out of the apartment she shared with us. At the time Mark had asked Jill if I was in a relationship, and she told him I was married.

He would later tell me, "You didn't seem married."

I wouldn't say Mark cornered me in the living room; more like everyone else wandered off to do some job and left the two of us standing there, maid of honor and best man, too big for the suburban décor. A couple of toddlers played at our feet. The whole domestic scene would have made me cringe, except that he was telling an interesting story: His boat had just won third place in the Venetian Night parade.

Every July, a million people (literally, a million people) flock to the downtown lakefront to watch the armada of bells and whistles. Mark's boat, adorned in a Blues Brothers theme, had won the Mayor's Vote with its painted set, elaborate light show, blues singers, dancers, and Jake and Elwood.

Head down, rifling through photos on his phone, Mark said, "I have to show you the dancing nun." Did he know my mom had been a nun? Did he know I wrote my first novel about nuns? Was this some weird sort of pickup line?

He handed me the phone. I squinted to see the boat, and a tall man dressed in a full habit.

"That's cool." I handed it back to him.

He smiled, thrilled at his boat's accomplishment. His blue eyes seemed overly large and intense; it was a little unnerving when they looked right at me.

"I live on it," he said. "It's my home."

He lived on his boat? Was that even possible? In Chicago, winter temperatures plunge to single digits for a long stretch in January and February. Could you really just plunk down your boat wherever you wanted and *live* on it?

As intriguing as it sounded, I was antsy to get away, afraid that I would get stuck talking to the best man about his boat all afternoon. I politely excused myself. Most people still hadn't arrived, so Mark turned to the next logical guests: He got down on the floor and played trucks with the toddlers. No single guy I knew played with kids.

Later, the party in full swing, I found myself sitting beside him outside, eating barbecue. He told some good jokes. I told him about a feature story I had just finished on the Cook County coroner's office. There was one employee I really wanted to talk to but couldn't reach; when we finally talked, he told me how he had grown up down the street from the morgue. He had always loved death.

"You know why he was so hard to get ahold of?" I asked. "His mom is dying."

"Ah," Mark said. "There's the story."

He was right; that was the story. I hadn't been able to get that into the article and I was dissatisfied with the final piece. But Mark got it.

A little later, during the gift opening, I looked over and smiled at him, and he smiled back. It was a knowing smile, like we were in on some secret together.

A month passed. A boring date with the architect elicited no follow-up call. The reporter kissed my hand and left my apartment when I told him it was off. The temp went on a drinking binge and disappeared.

I drove to Detroit for the wedding. I was single, and though a wedding was all the excuse I needed to get good and drunk (as if I needed any excuse that summer), I was well aware that I should be on my best behavior, lest I embarrass my best friend in front of her new family. I was also aware that as the only single woman in this wedding party, there could be scheming to hook me up with one of the groom's single friends. All summer I'd been attending weddings, and this seemed to be the way things were done. I liked the attention, but I was wary of the outcomes, particularly if stories got back to Jill or her new family. In my mind, wedding hookups were always a little seedy. Nobody ever meets her future spouse at a wedding.

On the eve of the nuptials, Jill went to bed early, and Scott took the rest of us out for a boat ride on one of the lakes dotting the Detroit suburbs.

The August night was warm, the lake lit by a full moon. We cruised around, then pulled up to a dock, stripped down to our underwear, and jumped overboard into perfect late-summer lake water.

Under the water, dark and colder near the bottom, I swam out farther. When I came up for air and turned around to look toward shore, there was someone behind me, treading water. I was expecting one of the groom's friends—but it was Mark, smiling at me. The kindness in his face surprised me.

The next day during the ceremony, I looked over at the best man through my tears. In my summer of weddings I had watched plenty of groomsmen rolling their eyes during the ceremony, poking one another and joking. But Mark—he was actually listening.

At the reception, I took my plate from the buffet and went to the head table, where the bride and groom were chatting it up. I sat with them, but quickly they were whisked away for photos, leaving me alone. I did not want to be sitting alone at a wedding. At a table behind me, Mark sat with a woman who looked like she could be his aunt.

"You should be at the head table," I told them. "Come sit over here."

So the two of them moved over one table, and Mark introduced me to his first-grade teacher, Sister Susan.

We were soon called for photos with the bride and groom on the veranda. The four of us stood together, smiling, and then suddenly the whole family gathered around us—all nine brothers and sisters, spouses, and kids. I was engulfed in somebody else's family wedding photo.

"Do you want me to go?" I asked Jill.

"No," she said, "you're my maid of honor—I want you to stay."

So I stayed at her side. Mark moved to my other side. The wedding photo shows about forty smiling, happy family members, with Mark and me standing together. We barely knew each other.

Later in the afternoon, when Mark gave the best-man speech wearing shorts and his Hawaiian shirt and standing on a picnic table, Jill's aunt Karen turned to me. "What about him?" she asked.

"Not my type," I said. He wasn't. He was at least ten years older than me, probably more. He looked like a real man who had a real job and wore ties to work and paid his bills on time. He was kind, polite, and introduced me to his first-grade teacher. He seemed so quiet and unassuming. His eyes were intense, but other than that, he seemed like a very nice man.

I was not interested in very nice men.

"Well, there's something there," she said, then added, "They're good people. They're *water* people."

At brunch the next morning, while Jill and Scott opened presents in their backyard, I prepared to leave early and drive friends to the airport. I made my way around the guests to say good-bye, and when I got to Mark, he and I made casual plans, when we both returned to Chicago, to get a group of friends together. Then he kissed me, full on the lips.

As I pulled away, I reasoned, *Well, maybe he's the kind of guy who kisses women on the lips; he does have a lot of sisters.*

Body Worlds was closing at the Museum of Science and Industry. Two weeks after the wedding, Mark arranged for a group of us to see the exhibit of human muscles riding horseback and ice skating, and the circulatory family holding hands. I parked my car and found Mark standing at the entrance, waiting. Most of the group was already inside. He was waiting for me.

We stood out in front talking, then went inside to meet everyone, waiting in line. It was an afternoon of waiting, during which Mark and I discovered we both loved Ben Franklin and traveling abroad alone. Once inside the crowded exhibit, our group fractured and we all wandered at our own pace. But I kept looking for him, among the muscles and arteries.

He was very good at this dating thing; I didn't even realize I was being courted. There was no formality to any of it. One evening, as I waited for a call from a guy I'd met online to come at precisely eight o'clock for our precise half-hour predate conversation, the phone rang and it was Mark. I relaxed and we chatted and I forgot all about the scheduled predate conversation. He'd called to say he was inviting some friends out on his boat for the last Saturday night of summer fireworks, and would I like to come along?

I arrived early, wearing a short black skirt, black sleeveless shirt, black hiking sandals. *Mazurka* was docked just outside the wall of the Chicago River at River City Marina, just south of the Loop, in a maze of condos and warehouses where you would never expect to find a marina or even a river, for that matter.

"You're the first to arrive," he said, walking me from the parking garage through the back delivery alley, and out to a small marina. We passed a row of powerboats before arriving at his home.

Mazurka looked just the way I thought Mark's boat would look— square and sturdy, a classic style without being pretentious. It was white with blue canvas covering the flybridge, its many windows out-lined in teak.

A Marine Trader recreational trawler like *Mazurka* has a shape and sturdiness similar to the well-known fishing trawlers that pull nets ("trawls") through the water. Like a fishing trawler, *Mazurka* has a semi-displacement hull that, according to the Dictionary of English Nautical Language, "achieves buoyancy by displacing a volume of water equal to its weight. A design of a ship in which the displace-ment (the weight of a mass of water pushed aside by the intrusion of a ship's hull) does not change significantly as the vessel moves through the water."

Mazurka was born nearly thirty years earlier in Taiwan, thirty-eight feet long, with a mast and a V-shaped keel and a single Ford engine that pushed her at eight knots, top speed. She proudly wore her association's flag at the bow pulpit, MARINE TRAWLER OWNERS ASSOCIATION AMERICA, with its mascot, the turtle.

According to Jack Horner, writing for BoatU.S., recreational trawlers grew in popularity during the 1970s fuel crisis. As power-boaters got used to paying more for gas, the fast, fuel-loving speedboats took the limelight again, but now, as a generation of boaters grow older and want a slower pace and vessels that are easier to care for, trawlers have regained popularity.

One of the reasons for their popularity, Horner writes, is because "the designers have done an excellent job laying out an efficient deck area while, at the same time, maximizing interior space and accommodations."

The trawlers' design also makes them good for long-range cruising, and comfortable for liveaboards.

"Come on inside," Mark said, stepping from the cement wall to the side deck of his home. I followed him around the stern to the port side of the boat, right on the water. Across the river the post office hummed, and just north of us the Sears Tower (now called Willis Tower), one of the tallest buildings in the world, greeted me with a friendliness I had never seen in it before. Maybe it was the close proximity, unhindered by traffic and el platforms? It seemed to beckon me like a backyard neighbor: *Welcome to the neighborhood.*

Mark slipped through an open doorway and I followed him down a step into the main cabin, which is technically called the "saloon," though Mark has always called it the "salon," and I prefer his term. I could easily stand in the small room, only thirteen feet across, which served as living room and galley. The salon was nested with warm, toffee-colored teak everywhere. Because we were above the water, windows stretched around the perimeter, letting in the soft early-evening dusk and the reflection of skyscraper lights on the river. On every wall not covered by a window hung Navajo paintings. To the left of the doorway, there was an L-shaped, canvas-covered bench curved around a table; opposite the door was a small galley—a sink, a three-burner stove, a tiny refrigerator, and a counter supporting a gigantic microwave. The shelf beside the microwave was overflowing with cereal boxes, cans of black olives, crackers, and sardines. In front of the refrigerator sat a rather large, flat-leafed plant. To its right, at a forty-five-degree angle from the door, stood a shelf filled with liquor. And the other shelves—to the right of the door, behind the bench, at the bow—were stuffed with all kinds of random items: magazines, binoculars, mail, flashlights, candles, keys, walkie-talkies, tools.

Tools burst from everywhere.

"I'm right in the middle of a project," Mark said, apologizing for the wrenches and screwdrivers scattered on the floor. I wondered if he knew guests were coming. "Here, let me show you the head."

He turned to the stern and stepped down into a stateroom, where a queen-sized bed with a beautiful, multicolored quilt took up most of the room. Navajo paintings and weavings covered the walls. He opened a narrow door to his left and showed me the bathroom, complete with a tiny bathtub and shower. "Here's the toilet," he said, pointing to the low stool. "Put your toilet paper in the garbage. After you go, you flush it like this"—he pumped the side lever a few times, water filling the tank. "That's it."

We returned to the salon, Mark shaking his head. "Tools everywhere," he said, "I have such a mess." He knelt down near the bow, beside an electrical panel. "There's another stateroom up here," he said, nodding to the dark room behind him. "I keep fishing gear up here now. And another bathroom." He began arranging the piles at his knees. "If you want, you can go ahead up top and write, or whatever you want. Make yourself at home. I need to clean up."

I liked his style—unpretentious, a little chaotic, attentive to those around him.

When Mark released me to explore the boat on my own, I took my notebook and went out to the foredeck, where the Sears Tower still winked at me. I skirted around the starboard side, via the side deck, peeking inside one of the many windows to see Mark kneeling, carefully placing tools in a large red box. At the stern, I climbed the few steps onto the aft deck, then the short ladder up to the flybridge, which covered the salon.

The flybridge featured the helm with a large silver wheel and two swivel chairs. Scattered around were more plastic chairs and a large cooler. I sat and tried to write but didn't know what to say. I had lived in Chicago ten years but had never been on the river. Atop the flybridge, the city was almost completely silent. I had never imagined this kind of Chicago.

Oddly enough, as I stepped aboard *Mazurka* the first time, I felt at home. I had grown up on boats. True, they were twelve-foot aluminum fishing boats that my dad took us out on every weekend on the northern backwaters of the Mississippi River, but I was a River Rat from way back nonetheless. I knew how to stand in a boat, how to pull a boat through water, and to keep my fingers inside the boat when we approached a dock. *Mazurka*, I reasoned, was just a larger version of what I had been riding my whole life.

Mark's other guests arrived and we embarked, bound for Navy Pier. On the way up the river, we passed the Sears Tower, the Merchandise Mart, the Tribune Tower, and the Wrigley Building. "See that one over there," Mark said, pointing to a skyscraper with Greek-style pillars. "That's all done with lights. There are no pillars."

As we passed under the final bridge and neared Lake Michigan, we came upon a fleet of boats waiting at the end of the river for the lock to open. Navy Pier, that mile-long tourist trap, jutted out just north of us; the Loop skyscrapers hid the setting sun just behind. Mark passed around the mandatory life jackets. A horn sounded, the lock doors opened, the red light turned to green, and our procession of boats filed into the lock—first the *Summer of George* and the *Ouilmette* crammed with tourists, and then the smaller boats like us, and even some tiny fishing boats, sidling up to the wall. Mark handed me a long boat hook to grab onto the wall and we held our position steady as the doors closed behind us.

As a kid I had toured Lock and Dam 15 on the Mississippi plenty of times, watching tugboats push huge barges through the changing water levels. This was the first time I ever actually went through a lock. It was exhilarating to enter that dangerous, precarious hold be-

tween river and lake. I wondered how much the water level would change and held tightly to the wall with my hook, ready for a six-foot drop. As the doors closed behind us I felt the pull of the water; the rise in water level was barely perceptible, but there was no question that everything had changed. Then the doors to the lake opened, releasing us into the limitless expanse of Lake Michigan.

A parking lot of boats had gathered for the last fireworks of the season. Mark settled *Mazurka* as close to the fireworks platform as the police boats would allow. While we waited for the show to begin, I took a break from conversation on the flybridge to wander down to the deck at the bow. Suddenly a huge explosion in front of us erupted as fireworks exploded right over our heads. I sat down on the bow to watch the show, alone. It was lovely.

As we headed back to River City at the end of the night, we sat atop the flybridge, tranquil and tired, the early-fall breeze blowing on our bare skin, the gentle lull of the boat as she cleaved through the water. Mark gave the wheel to one of his friends and came back to sit beside me. He was relaxed, at perfect ease on the water, and brighter to me than anything else around him. I was surprised how easy it was to talk with him. For once, I wasn't trying to be somebody else.

A week later, we went out on a real date. Just the two of us. No more group dates to see if we actually liked each other. This was the real deal. Mark bought two tickets to a one-man show about Chopin at the Royal George Theatre. We agreed to meet at the theater. Around five o'clock I called him at his office to find out how he was getting to the theater. We worked on the same university campus, just two buildings apart. He was a pharmacy professor, I was a writer for the nursing school.

"Why don't I give you a ride," he said. I agreed.

"Oh, by the way," he added, "I have my bike."

"Bike?"

"Motorcycle. Have you been on a motorcycle before?"

I paused. I didn't want to seem unadventurous. "No," I confessed.

"It's fun—you'll be fine. Meet me at the parking garage."

I hung up the phone and wandered out to the hall where some colleagues were chatting at the end of the day. "I'm going on a date," I told them, "and he's driving me on his motorcycle."

"That's great!" one officemate declared. "My husband has a motorcycle. You'll love it. But you can't go like that—" She looked at my short black skirt. "Here, let's get you some scrubs." Off she went, rifling through one of the student nursing closets, emerging with green scrub pants. "Wear these."

My skirt in my purse, I traipsed across campus in a polka-dotted blouse, black heels, and green scrub pants. At the parking garage, I found Mark gearing up a 1986 Honda Gold Wing. It's a huge bike, which didn't necessarily make me feel any safer. He handed me a helmet. "Now, one thing you should know. When we go around a curve, it will feel like the bike is going to tip over. It's not going to tip over."

"Thanks for the warning," I said, growing more nervous by the minute.

He climbed on the bike and without much grace I figured out how to throw my leg over and sit behind him. It felt way too intimate to be straddling a huge motorcycle, and I wasn't entirely comfortable putting my arms around him. My suddenly prim attitude? Maybe the fact that he was my best friend's brother-in-law. Or that he was older, a real man. Mark seemed too clean-cut for me, too wholesome. And despite the quirkiness of living on a boat, he appeared very conservative. But really—the truth, I think, is that he wasn't my type. I didn't want a relationship with him, and I didn't want to lead him on. Yet there I was, and the second we pulled onto the Eisenhower Expressway and zoomed toward downtown, the pavement racing at seventy miles an hour just inches beneath my heels, I wrapped my arms around him and hung on for dear life.

Under the post office we went, along Congress to the lakefront, then up Lake Shore Drive. At the curve just north of the John Hancock, grateful for the warning, I squeezed Mark's waist and shut my eyes tight as we rounded the bend at well over the speed limit, practically on our side. Once we were upright again, I screamed and laughed. He patted my hand in a gesture far more intimate than any one-night stand.

At the theater, while Mark got our tickets from the box office, I changed into my skirt in the bathroom. We had an hour before the performance and decided to go a few doors down to an Italian restaurant.

As we waited for dinner, we discussed our travels—Mark had bicycled through Thailand and France, Alaska and the western United States; I had spent six weeks in Russia, traveled in France and England, road-tripped with Jill seven thousand miles through the U.S. Neither of us had been to Italy. "To Italy," Mark said, toasting, looking over his glass of Chianti at me.

In the theater, just before curtain, he turned to me. "I wonder if he'll play a mazurka?" The actor came out and began the show with one of the famous waltzes Mark's boat was named for.

I was sitting quite comfortably, enjoying the performance, when suddenly the strangest feeling of peace came over me. I glanced at Mark, sitting there in his khaki work pants and short sleeves and tie. I barely knew him.

After the finale, the actor came back for an encore; out of character, he talked about the end of Chopin's evenings in parlor rooms, when everyone would sing together. So for the encore we had a sing-along—a whole theater, mostly full of people older than my parents, and Mark and me—all singing.

I imprinted the scene in my mind because I wanted to keep it with me for the rest of my life: It was the moment I fell in love.

Less than a week later we went on our second date, slicing down the cavernous river between walls of glass and steel. It amazed me that the city I had known for more than a decade could be so quiet, so private, so *spacious*.

There was a sushi restaurant up the river that Mark wanted to try. We motored up the river to the north branch, where he suddenly pulled up to the wall in front of a swanky restaurant. Fancy-dressed people poured out the doors, cocktails in hand. With no dock in sight, beside signs announcing NO DOCKING, he tied up to the wall. We hopped the railing in our jeans and sweatshirts; young guys in overpriced suits smoking cigars nodded respect. The hostess led us past the bar, past the chichi girls wearing tank tops and fake tans, posing with cosmos, past most of the restaurant to the very last seats at the sushi bar, beside the kitchen door.

I confessed my hesitancy to get involved with him. "You seem too . . . conservative for me."

He lay down his chopsticks and leaned closer to me, peering at me with those blue eyes. "We could have a lot of fun together."

The quiet, unassuming veneer was only a cover for the impulsive risk taker who lay just under the surface.

After dinner, we hopped the railing and climbed back on board. The cigar smokers helped us push off, admiring the boat.

We retraced our journey from the week before, cruising down the river, out the lock at Navy Pier, then motoring around to the calm enclosure in front of the John Hancock building. Boaters nicknamed it "the playpen" for its smooth waters and floating summer parties. It's not unusual to see six or seven boats rafted together on a Saturday afternoon, music blaring.

We brought up sleeping bags and lay them out atop the flybridge, in front of the city, under the watchful eye and broad shoulders of the Hancock. I couldn't imagine sleeping outside in the city under any circumstances, and it felt thrilling—even a little risky—to lie beside Mark with the sky open all around us, the late-night traffic humming along the curve of Lake Shore Drive. This boat, I realized, gave us permission to go anywhere we wanted, do anything we wanted.

Very early the next morning—as the sun was just peeking over the horizon—Mark woke me and helped me stumble down to the stateroom, where he tucked me into his bed. "I'm going to take us back to the marina," he said, pulling up the blankets around me. Half asleep, I tentatively breathed in the scent of his sheets (a woman can always tell by her nose, and a perfectly good man can be checked off because his scent is not conducive to our own): It smelled of clean laundry, with just a tinge of diesel, oil, and sweat. A warm smell, a workingman. I settled down into the bed and fell into a deep sleep, all the way back to River City.

MAFIA MAN

~~~~~~

There are more than nine thousand restaurants in Chicago; Mark and I seemed intent on trying all of them.

This alerted my provincial father. "I'd keep an eye out," he said. "Knows all the best restaurants, lives on a boat . . . probably got mafia ties."

In response, I emailed him Mark's curriculum vitae, detailing sixteen years of an academic career in the health sciences. "Not a mafia guy," I assured him, "but just as unusual."

Mark was unconventional from the get-go, a paradox in action. By day, he was a disorganized professor; by night and weekends, he was a man's man, conquering the elements, climbing rock and ice, gnawing raw steak off a T-bone, and living on his boat in the third largest city in the country.

I couldn't get enough of him.

For the past two centuries of documented history, people on the fringes of Chicago have found all kinds of reasons to live on its waterways. In the nineteenth century, ship captains and crews spent winters on the vessels they sailed in the summer. During the Great Depression, houseboats became an economical alternative to life on land—many of them moored along the North Branch of the Chicago River after the Sanitary District of Chicago finished the channeling project. Liveaboards could avoid real estate taxes and pull up anchor whenever they needed—while some of them rarely moved at all.

In the 1940s, a booming downtown was just beginning its sky-scraper revolution. The nautical homes of liveaboards—rundown shacks with tarpaper sides and tiny stovepipes—floated beneath the North Side Bridge at Irving Park Boulevard. The residents on land were none too happy with their non-tax-paying neighbors. *Why do they have to live on water? What are they up to that they can't live like everybody else? What exactly goes on down there, anyway?*

These boats—often the bottoms of barges that had been used for hauling until they wore out—were swept and tidy, displaying flower boxes and curtains in the windows. A little shed held a pile of coal to keep the liveaboards warm in winter by heating the tiny, low-ceilinged rooms. One woman who lived on the east bank for several years kept an array of electric floor lamps and wall fixtures, though they had no light bulbs, nor electricity, for that matter.

(When you live on a boat, there is always the chance that someday you will head back to land. Better stock up on things you'll need, like lamps.)

Chicago met its most infamous liveaboard—not surprisingly a scoundrel of sorts—when "Cap" George Wellington Streeter, a former Mississippi riverboat captain, ran his thirty-five-ton steamboat, the *Reutan*, onto a sandbar off the shoreline near East Superior Street during a storm on July 10, 1886. As he couldn't budge the ship, he decided to stay. In the mass cleanup after the Great Fire, people threw debris in the lake; Cap Streeter welcomed everybody to dump their garbage near his moored ship, and soon his homestead increased to 186 acres of landfill, reaching the Chicago shoreline. Cap Streeter claimed this as the independent "United States District of Lake

Michigan," not subject to the laws of Chicago or Illinois. He began issuing deeds to other pioneers like himself.

Anyone attempting to remove Cap Streeter or the squatters would be run off with gunfire, axes, or pots of scalding water. Sometimes these raids resulted in Cap Streeter's arrest for assault; often he was let off for acting in self-defense. Once he was acquitted because buckshot was not considered deadly.

In 1890, industrialist N. K. Fairbank sued Streeter, claiming the land was his, and he won. Nonetheless, Cap Streeter kept his hold on the land, a sort of Streeter shantytown, where you could buy liquor and prostitutes, and shack up for the night if you needed a place to stay.

Today Cap Streeter's shantytown has been renamed "Streeterville" and is one of the priciest pieces of real estate in the city, sitting smack between the Magnificent Mile and the lake, north of the Chicago River. On the landfill created by the Great Fire, you can tour the Museum of Contemporary Art, buy an overpriced studio condo with a lake view, and see a doctor at Northwestern University Hospital. Some things never change; Streeterville's swanky hotels house today's pioneers: those who shop.

These were the forefathers of the man I was falling in love with? Outlaws, scoundrels, and destitutes?

Truth be told, I sorta liked the idea.

The oldest of nine children, Mark grew up in one of the least densely populated parts of this country, the Keweenaw Peninsula, at the very tip of Michigan's Upper Peninsula, where "yoopers" hunt rabbit, deer, and bear, and fish for trout in Lake Superior. On a clear day, you can see Canada in the distance while you cut down your Christmas tree in the woods. Three hundred inches of snow fall in the winter, and people build raised sidewalks of planks to their front doors. Every town has a shop that sells pasties and every third house has a "sow-na." When Mark was growing up in the 1960s and '70s, the nearest fast-food restaurant was a hundred miles away.

After graduating from pharmacy school, Mark headed west to work with the Public Health Service on a Navajo reservation in Chinle, Arizona, where he spent five years riding his bike on the mesa and skiing the Four Corners. He traveled to Kentucky for graduate school, took a fellowship in Kansas City, Missouri, did more work in Kentucky, and then one day in his early thirties found himself standing on Michigan Avenue. The position at the university sounded good; he knew he would be staying.

But where does a yooper live in the third largest city in the country?

He started with a small apartment in Rogers Park, the farthest neighborhood on the North Side of Chicago, bordering the lake to the east and Evanston to the north. Rogers Park is one of the most diverse neighborhoods in the city—in 2001 there was an equal blend of white, black, and Hispanic residents, and everyone else between. Students from Loyola University mix with gangbangers on Morse Avenue. One block can be a different culture from the next, and if you come home after 7 p.m. to the rows of apartment houses filling the east side, be ready to drive around for an hour to find a parking spot.

One evening after work, Mark took his golden retriever Coffee for a walk. He stopped by the drugstore and left Coffee outside, untied, at halt. Coffee was an obedient dog and knew to stay, but when Mark came out, Coffee was gone. Mark roamed up and down the blocks, yelling, "Coffee! Coffee!" to the strange looks of pedestrians. "No, I don't want any coffee," one guy told him. Mark posted signs on trees promising a reward, and shortly afterward he got a call. He took fifty dollars to the apartment of an exotic dancer. "I like your dog," she told him. "She got along well with my snake."

On another walk, Mark and Coffee heard the screeching of a van coming down the block; it halted just short of them, a door opened, and bullets erupted from within, pelting the apartment doors and windows. Mark and Coffee hit the sidewalk. In less than a minute, the van was gone. A few weeks later, so were Mark and Coffee.

As Mark was moving out of Rogers Park, I was moving onto the very same street—just one block closer to the lake. I was going to graduate school downtown at the time, taking the el home late at night, and stayed about the same amount of time. One weekday around noon a kid was shot in front of my apartment. Teenagers in red converged and lingered for a full thirty minutes before the ambulance arrived. I moved out.

It would be nine more years before we met.

Next came Lakeview for Mark, a few miles south of Rogers Park, bordering the lake and home to Wrigley Field. Lakeview, with its clean, neighborly streets and good restaurants, its rainbow-colored flags and rowdy, drunken Cubs fans. One morning Mark emerged from his apartment to find that after the Cubs game the night before, someone had walked over every car parked on his block, including his Mitsubishi 3000GT, leaving footprints and dents and some vomit at the end.

In the six years Mark lived in Lakeview, he didn't spend too much time in the neighborhood; his work required more energy than he had to give, and he would leave early in the morning and come home late at night. He soon decided that his job was the problem, and a career change would make him happy. Medical school was the answer, and to save money he gave away his furniture and his apartment and moved in with a friend living in Evanston. He started saving money and studying for the MCAT, but before even sitting for the exam he realized that he would be racking up massive debt for a career he would not even be able to begin until he was in his mid-forties. He abandoned the idea of medical school and started looking for the next place to live.

It was the beginning of a new century, and everyone was approved to buy the condo of their dreams. Parents of college students were buying condos as investments. Students were using education loans to buy condos. People with four other properties were buying condos. We were at war and you couldn't go wrong in buying property, even if that property was a spot in the sky with four walls and carpeting. The whole city of Chicago was buying condos, and Mark, in his final attempt to fit into the urban landscape, jumped on the bandwagon. Buying a condo would finally allow him to fit in with everybody else. Buying a condo would make him happy.

Thus began the parade of real estate agents.

Real Estate Agent #1 showed him a studio in Lakeview, not too expensive, and with a forty-thousand-dollar parking space on concrete marked by paint. "I just couldn't see myself getting into this studio with a forty-thousand-dollar parking space." She found him another place he liked, and he told her to put a bid on it. She didn't, and it sold. "I was mad at her, so I got rid of her."

Mark then got the idea that maybe he should buy a three-flat and rent out two of the flats and make some money on his investment.

Real Estate Agent #2 showed him a three-flat in the Pilsen neighborhood. There were chickens running around the yard and a rooster crowing. "I imagined myself living in the attic of one of these three-flats and managing the tenants. I wasn't sure I wanted to be a landlord in this neighborhood with chickens. I gave up the idea."

Real Estate Agent #3 showed Mark a place he really liked in Evanston, but he got cold feet. "Even the Realtor's husband called me and said, 'Man, you should get this place, this is a place you could raise a family in.' I think that scared me because I was single. It looked too domestic for me. I decided I wasn't going to get it, even though it was probably the best place I could have gotten. I put the nix on it. Then she fired me."

By this time, Mark was spending weekends on his twenty-six-foot boat, the *Escape Hatch*, appropriately named, "because I was looking for an escape and it served me well."

Mark started boating in Chicago by chance. Five years prior, he had left the Mitsubishi with his brother Ed in the UP for some repair. While Ed worked on the car, he gave Mark his jeep to drive (I've never seen such generous trading and loaning as goes on in this family), and a bonus—the family boat, eloquently named the *Lund*. A fifteen-foot fiberglass boat that looked very similar to the boats I had grown up fishing in, the *Lund* had been in their family for three decades, and now Mark was bringing it from the UP to Chicago.

He parked the *Lund* in a friend's driveway for a week until he figured out where he could keep it. Most marinas in Chicago didn't take boats that small, but South Branch Marina, hiding just beneath the Dan Ryan Expressway next to a cement company, was glad to take the boat. Soon Mark was learning to navigate the Chicago River and Lake Michigan in a tiny fiberglass fishing craft with an outboard motor. Mark and Scott made a movie of their adventures aboard the *Lund*. One shot shows them on a summer evening idling on the Chicago River in front of the Merchandise Mart, Mark at the stern, playing his homemade dulcimer; you can just hear the twangy folk sounds over the outboard motor as huge tour boats pass behind him. Another shot is taken later that night from the boat just off Navy Pier, downtown Chicago floating up and down as the brothers rise and dip in the lake.

"Where are the fireworks going off?" Scott asks.

"Here," Mark says.

"Where?"

"Here, right here."

You can't help but think these two are crazy for taking a tiny fishing boat out with the powerboats and ships circling Navy Pier, watching fireworks shoot off right over them, and you would be right; the video location abruptly changes and the next scene shows them across the country at Mount Rainier, gearing up to ascend the fourteen-thousand-foot mountain.

Mark passed the *Lund* to his brother John and moved up to the *Escape Hatch*, a 1977 Chris-Craft single-engine runabout boat that had a bed and a sink in the cabin. He bought it from a guy in Marquette, Michigan, who used it less than half a dozen times, ran out of gas with it in Lake Superior, and almost sank it after running it up on a breakwall. The *Escape Hatch* became Mark's means of learning Chicago waterways; he explored the North and South Branches of the Chicago River, and he learned how to drive a boat with a single-propeller inboard motor.

More and more often, first on weekends and then on weeknights, Mark would drive over to South Branch Marina. He would ask the "boat valet" (an operator with a forklift) to bring his boat down from the racks and put it in the water. He'd visit his new friend, Linda, who ran the hot dog stand and was like a second mother to him, who first made him hot dogs and hamburgers and then his favorite steak so he could eat dinner on the river after work.

Living in the city with so many people was always a challenge, but the river and Lake Michigan kept Mark in Chicago. Going out on the water was calm and peaceful—it was a wilderness. "I wanted to engage the city on my terms. My terms were to view the city without having to get out of the way of someone. With my boat, I could go where I wanted, throw an anchor down, and just sit there and watch it. The water was a little haven away from all the crime, dirt, and noise, where I could see the beauty of the city instead of being in the thick of it. You can't see how beautiful it is when you are right in the middle of it."

He began to realize that his dream place would be along the river, where he could walk out of his home, jump on his boat, and cruise away. It was boating that brought him closest to nature in the city; that's where he was happiest.

One night, having gone through three real estate agents and more than thirty condos, Mark was driving back to his friend's Evanston home after spending a weekend on the *Escape Hatch* when a new idea occurred to him.

"I was thinking about my friend Cindy who lived aboard a thirty-eight-foot Chris-Craft on the river. She was getting married and selling her boat." He called her and she told him living on a boat was no problem, that winters were manageable. Then she said the magic words that cinch the deal for every future liveaboard: "If I can do this, so can you."

Fueled by childhood television dreams of Quincy and the fantasy of living on a boat, Mark began searching the want ads. Specifically for a trawler, which he reasoned would be sturdy and survive the winter. He looked at half a dozen boats and then one rainy Saturday morning came across an ad for *Mazurka*. From the picture, he knew it was his boat. He jumped on his motorcycle and rode up in the rain to Waukegan, where the broker told him that he couldn't look at the boat just then because people were living on it, but if he wanted to make a deposit they could hold it for him. Mark plunked down five hundred dollars to secure the boat and then had to wait two weeks to see it. In those two weeks, he worried whether or not this was the boat of his dreams. The picture was perfect, the price was perfect, but the listing left out a lot of details. Did it have a bow thruster? It was a big boat; how was he going to maneuver it to a dock without a bow thruster? Did it have a generator? Did it have any electronics at all, or was it just a bare-bones trawler?

Mark finally saw *Mazurka* on the Saturday of Chaos. His sister Aimee, her husband Ken, and their little toddler Miriam were visiting Chicago; Ken was running the Chicago Marathon that day but left his race chip in Appleton, Wisconsin; Ken went off to run the marathon; Mark had an eighteen-year-old cat, Putty Cat, who was dying; he had her put to sleep that morning; Little Miriam let out the cats at Mark's friend's house in Evanston; Mark, Aimee, and Miriam put up signs all over the neighborhood for the missing cats; Mark packed his recently deceased Putty Cat on the back of his motorcycle because he planned to bury her at Kettle Moraine, Wisconsin, where he'd buried Coffee several years earlier; Mark drove his motorcycle (deceased cat on the back) up to Racine, Wisconsin, to see the boat; on the way, the broker called him to say, "You won't believe this—the boat has everything you were asking about *and more!*"; Aimee and Miriam drove up in their car; Ken was still running the marathon; the owner of *Mazurka* yelled at Aimee and refused to let kids on his boat or even on the dock; Aimee and Miriam drove off; Mark boarded *Mazurka* and took her for a test drive on Lake Michigan; while driving the boat for the first time, his friend from Evanston called, hysterical about her missing cats; back at the harbor, Mark finally met up with Aimee, Ken, and Miriam; the four of them drove out to Kettle Moraine and found the spot where Coffee was buried; they dug a hole for Putty Cat and had a ceremony; Mark drove his motorcycle back to Chicago, praying that his friend's cats had returned; they had.

Somewhere in here, Mark decided this was the boat of his dreams and made an offer. Another two weeks of haggling followed, in which he almost walked away from the deal, but in the end, *Mazurka* became his.

Around the time Mark bought *Mazurka* and became an official liveaboard, he started making a concerted effort to date. He was in his early forties, a confirmed bachelor, and ready for something more serious.

Living on a boat makes dating . . . interesting. Mark's friend Jay told him, "It's like owning a Ferrari. It's cool to own a Ferrari. It's not cool to live in it."

According to Mark, "That sums up the dating thing."

Within the first week of dating Mark, I told him I was in love with him.

I can be prone to high drama and emotional extremes and the romance of romance, but it was true: I was in love with him. I didn't know this was the man I was looking for until he appeared in front of me, in his short-sleeved dress shirt and tie and oil-stained khakis. He was a doctor in psychiatric pharmacology with a penchant for fixing engines. The table beside his pillow displayed a thick reading pile: the expected boating magazines, *PassageMaker*, *BoatU.S.*; *The Wall Street Journal* and *Smithsonian* magazine; a thick, well-read *Don Quixote*; and the Catholic Office of the Hours, which he prayed in the morning and at night.

I didn't know a combination of all these qualities could exist in one person until there he was, briefcase in one hand and bowline in the other, telling me hop aboard, let's motor down to the Lyric Opera and try to get scalped tickets for *La Traviata*.

He was a paradox in action, and I was usually delighted at each unexpected turn. One minute he's sneaking me into the River City parking so I don't have to pay, and the next he's saying, "If we're going to be in a relationship, we're going to have to learn how to pray together." Which is what he told me one afternoon during a lunch break, in the campus square between our two buildings, as we sat terribly close together. I almost jumped up and ran. *Pray* together? I prayed, yes; I was an adamant prayer, and had been since I was a kid with terrible nighttime anxiety attacks. But prayer was something done alone, unless it was an Our Father during church. Even the Rosary seemed too personal to pray in a group. But actual *prayer*— like, a conversation with God? In the presence of another person? Forget it.

From the very start, *Mazurka* was a part of our love affair. Unlike the women his dating service matched him with, I loved that he lived on a boat. It was so strange that it made perfect sense. Not wild about cramped city condos or suburban strip malls? Make your own solution: Live on a boat.

On a fall Sunday afternoon, we took *Mazurka* out around Navy Pier, just inside the curve at Oak Street Beach where triathletes train for open-water swims in cold Lake Michigan. In front of the Han-

cock, we dropped anchor, cooked burgers on the fantail grill off the stern, and lay on the aft deck, listening to music and watching the clouds pass overhead. Later, we washed dishes and read and made Sunday family calls on our cell phones, both of us talking to our moms and brothers and sisters. I tried not to eavesdrop, from where I stood washing plates at the galley sink, but I couldn't help hearing Mark's voice five feet away and a few steps down in the aft stateroom. He was talking to Scott, who must have asked what the weather was like. "It's great," Mark told him. I heard him go to the window and pull back the curtain. "I mean, it's overcast and raining a little, and a little cold, but it's great." Yep, we had both been struck with love.

Looking out the rainy windows before me, I had a clear view of the downtown skyline, so full of people and so quiet. Out alone on the water, isolated, with all the wonderful things about the city right in front of us, I wondered, *Does he think it's strange that he can share*

his life with me like this? That I can come onto his boat and be perfectly happy and content and even like *it as much as he does?*

It seemed the most natural thing in the world to spend so much time on the water. My friend Anne, an astrologer, would say that's because I have so much water in my chart. A Scorpio sun sign and a Pisces Ascendant (with a Gemini moon thrown in for variety), of course I would be drawn to water. Sometimes I like to think this is true. Whether based on the stars and planets or the earth's geography, I have always sought water. There are photos of me swimming with my mom at the Y when I am six months old and instructors still encouraged parents to plunge their babies underwater. My dad tells a story of one afternoon when he was fishing in a deep channel bordering his sister's northern Wisconsin backyard. He decided to play a trick on his four-year-old daughter. "Watch this," he told my mom, setting his cigarettes and lighter on the dock. A fish the size of Jonah's whale suddenly took his line and yanked him into the water. I have no memory of this, but my dad tells me I thought it was so funny that I jumped into the water after him, scraping my chin on the dock and laughing all the way. He swam over and quickly grabbed me. "You weren't scared at all," he says, "you didn't even know how to swim."

This tendency to plunge in and figure out logistics later never left. If it looks fun, I'll jump. I don't need to know how to swim; I'll figure it out on the way to the bottom.

I felt I had nothing to hide from Mark—not my habit of eating sardines for dinner or my disdain for cleaning my bathroom. He observed and perceived rather than judged, unlike me, who was quick and impulsive and made rash decisions I might later regret. I tear off the wrapping paper 'cause I can't wait to see what's inside; Mark hems and haws a bit, examining the box from all angles before deciding how to best open it, then uses a tool like an X-Acto knife to do the job right. Had he been standing on the lawn that afternoon my dad was pulled in by a fish, Mark would have looked around for a few long minutes before spotting the canoe in the next yard over, then paddled out to save his future father-in-law from being eaten by a giant carp.

With Mark as my guide, I began to see water everywhere in the city, in places I had never noticed it before—while walking over the North Avenue Bridge between gentrified Wicker Park and the Cabrini Green projects, or crossing the Harrison Street Bridge on my way to the South Loop where I taught a writing workshop at Columbia College. And I began to see the city from the water. It no longer seemed so large, so overwhelming or indifferent. Rather, the skyscrapers looked like a giant chess pieces on a grid; the city became a game to be navigated. I realized this one afternoon as I rode on the back of Mark's motorcycle over the bridge at Navy Pier; "You're changing the way I see the city," I yelled, over the sound of the engine and his helmet.

He changed the way I see everything.

All dreamy-eyed romance aside, dating a lifelong bachelor who lives on a boat is not without its challenges.

I realized I was dating a confirmed bachelor on the morning when, after staying overnight on *Mazurka*, Mark left for work before I was out of his bed. I woke to find him gone. I dressed and packed my bag for work. When I tried to open the door, I found it shut tight.

I pulled and pushed: nothing.

There are three doors on *Mazurka*. The main door is on the port side, midship, entering the salon. The second door is on the starboard side, closer to the bow, slightly more narrow, and opening awkwardly into the interior helm, which is rarely used and mainly serves as an area for the ice machine, coatrack, and shelf for stacks of mail. The third door is a hatch on the aft deck, leading into the stateroom, opening just above the bed.

I tried to open the door again, but it wouldn't budge.

So I climbed over the icemaker and stacks of mail and out the starboard door, around the deck, to the portside door. It was closed tight and secured with the small brass lock in the shape of a Buddhist monk, a keyhole at his groin. Mark had gone to work and, forgetting he had a woman sleeping in his bed, locked his girlfriend inside his boat.

I went back to the starboard door and climbed back in for the small gold key, then back around to unlock the door so I could get out with my bag, late for work again.

Early in a romantic relationship (hell, maybe even after twenty years of marriage), women may be squeamish about using the bathroom with their new love interest in the next room. Particularly if that next room is separated by a paper-thin wall aboard a boat, where the slightest sigh travels like milk through cheesecloth, where the attentive captain on the other side is always listening for the slightest shift in sound, alerting him to potential trouble.

Basically, I couldn't do my business if Mark was around.

On another morning when I woke to find he had already left for work (do you sense a pattern here?), I got ready for the day in the usual way, but when I flushed the toilet, it wouldn't go down. I kept pumping the handle while the bowl filled with more and more water, almost reaching the top. I panicked.

Thus my first lesson in liveaboard life: *Adapt, overcome, improvise.* (Thanks to the Marine Corps and their unofficial motto.)

Petrified that Mark would come home to find shit soup in his bathroom, I ran to the galley for a plastic cup and knife. Carefully, I ladled the liquid down the bathtub drain. (Later, I learned that "gray water" from the sink and bathtub drains goes directly out of the boat. You're not even supposed to let the Chicago River water touch your skin, so it's not like I did major damage, but still . . .) With the knife, I chopped the waste into smaller bits and tried to flush again—no suction! The bowl filled with more water. I ladled more out until, mortified, helpless, and late yet again, I closed the lid on the toilet and left.

I called Mark from my office and warned him that the toilet was clogged. He later told me that by the time he got home, the bowl was empty—but who knows if he was only saying that to save my pride.

I was terrified of *Mazurka*'s septic system after that. I avoided the toilet, using it only in emergencies. Of course, a weekend on a boat can summon an emergency, and several weeks later I ran into the same situation—this time with Mark aboard. I closed the toilet lid and called for him. "Don't look inside," I told him, "just tell me what I need to do."

He came into the head. "You're not doing it right," he said. "You have to push the lever down to flush it—the way you're doing it just pumps water in."

It was my first indication—as if it wasn't obvious—that being with Mark would never resemble anything typical or "normal." I don't know that I ever considered myself normal, but I did do normal things, like go to work, call my mom on Sundays, live on land. If I had sewage problems, I did what any other young Chicago woman did: I panicked and paged the maintenance guys with ASAP urgency. My immediate comfort and privacy were A-1 priority.

But being with Mark was effortless. He got me and I got him. So he lived on a boat? I could make some minor adjustments and adapt while we were dating. I always had my apartment waiting for me when boat life got to be too much, and many Sunday nights I eagerly returned to my tiny sanctuary of steady floors and functioning plumbing.

Early on, we did have one fight, if you want to call a quiet, seemingly harmless discussion at Reza's followed by me leaving the table and hiding in the bathroom for half an hour a fight. We were eating in our fourth or fifth restaurant that week, sitting at the table in the elegant Middle Eastern dining room downtown, when we suddenly ran out of things to say. (If you're dating someone and this happens to you, don't panic. It's normal. Just eat your dinner.)

"Tell me a story," Mark said.

My mind went blank. A story? I may be a writer—a fiction writer, even—but tell you a story, off the cuff, just like that? My mind raced. I needed my laptop, my journal, a cup of coffee, and a long time to dawdle.

I think I said something to stall. Something like, "What kind of story?"

"Any story," he said eagerly. "Have you ever had a near-death experience?"

I thought about being twelve years old and climbing up some spring-flood-soaked bluffs near the backwaters of the Mississippi, someplace I was not supposed to be, someplace with rattlesnakes and a rumored burial ground, and someplace with spongy ground that didn't hold its trees very well; halfway up the hill, perched on a rock, I reached up to grasp a young tree and pulled it right out.

I told Mark this story. It didn't have much of an ending. There was only the briefest pause for drama. After a few seconds, I found another tree and hauled myself up.

"I don't know that many stories," I told him to account for his bored face. "I haven't had that much stuff happen to me."

"It's my fantasy to have some woman telling me stories," he said, "like in *Out of Africa*. He's a pilot and visits her and she tells him stories."

I agreed, it was a great fantasy. Except he was sitting with the wrong woman. I lived in Illinois, not Africa. I had never shot wild game, never protected the plantation from marauders. I'm not poetical like Baroness Karen von Blixen-Finecke or beautiful like Meryl Streep. I had spent seven years going to expensive schools for advanced degrees that only guaranteed me a lifetime of student loan debt. Stories? I sat in classrooms and read books. I rode around on el trains and imagined the secret lives of people sitting next to me. I had run a marathon, but so had half of Chicago. It had been a long time since I'd found a channel to jump into, and my impulsivity was going to waste, racking up student loan debt and sitting still.

Mark kept looking at me with such hope, and I was getting more flustered, feeling pushed to the wall, unable to account for my declared yet clearly preposterous profession. Who was I to call myself a writer when I couldn't even tell my man a story?

I escaped to the bathroom. It was empty, and I stood before the long row of sinks, talking myself down in the mirror. I wanted to leave. I wanted to run as far from this guy as I could. *Tell me a story.* What was I, some Persian restaurant jukebox? This isn't Arabian nights—you can't just feed me some dolma and out comes a story. For half an hour I nursed my poor, delicate ego, before finally coming to my senses that this whole thing was ridiculous and returning to the table.

But he was right: I didn't know how to tell a story.

I hadn't met the right audience. And I hadn't lived enough to know what a good story was.

Things were about to change.

RIVER RATS & OTHER RODENTS

The South Loop, *Mazurka*'s neighborhood at River City Marina, was in the midst of the biggest wave of gentrification the city had ever seen: Seven cranes anchored the skyline. New condos rose up on empty lots. The boat was within walking distance of the newest, biggest, glossiest Whole Foods in the city. There was even talk of the property just north—the beautiful green space that had survived the jackhammers and fat-fingered developers—finally breaking ground for—you guessed it—more condos.

Hadn't the housing market fallen through?

Developments like these made Mark nervous—he feared that one

day, the whole river would be developed and there wouldn't be any-where for liveaboards to spend the winter.

By that time, I reasoned, climate change would be in full effect, and the lake would be hospitable year-round.

Chicago—"The City That Works"—is a city of neighborhoods.

Chicagoans have figured out that if you want things to work, you have to work together. Every neighborhood has its association. Some are official, and powerful; there's the Triangle Association in Old Town, which represents the neighborhood's interests when a new hospital goes up, and stops private developers from tearing down his-toric homes to build mega-three-car garages for resale purposes. There are also the special-interest associations, like the Bucktown dog park club, which advocates for Bucktown's dog walkers and a well-cared-for dog park, adequate water and seating, and a new mural on the overpass. On Friday nights when other young Chicagoans are head-ing out to cocktail hour, the Bucktown dog park club heads home to collect their pooches and beverage of choice, then meet at the dog park for "dog-tail" hour.

And then there are the River Rats.

"River Rats & Other Rodents" (their official title) was a crew of hard-core liveaboards who wintered at the River City Marina. It was an eclectic group: a Chicago public school PE teacher, an NPR ad-dict, a City of Chicago union worker and his longtime girlfriend, an IRS employee, a dentist, a pharmacy professor, an engineer planning for retirement and sailing the world, and the unofficial mayor: Stan the Man.

Stan the Man was from Ireland, and usually drunk, though you'd never know it if you stayed out of breath-shot. He worked as a handyman with traveling carnivals for a while. How he ended up in Chicago living on a nameless Chris-Craft I don't know. He is the kind of guy who lives under the radar, always attached somehow to the main action; the kind of guy you believe has connections to politicians and mobsters, if only because he's willing to do the dirty work at the last minute and take the cash without asking questions.

He was also kind, friendly, and helpful to any boater. When a boat arrived in River City, Stan was right there to take the lines and tie up. Once, when Scott reached *Mazurka* ahead of us, Stan appeared, asking him who he was and why he was aboard *Mazurka*.

One night after midnight Mark and I came home to a quiet River City. We rounded the gates and passed along the dock's corridor, making just enough noise to scare away any rats. The water was quiet and still; the only sound was a subtle steam coming from the post office across the river. As we passed Stan's Chris-Craft, with Rice Krispies stashed in the window and mirrored letters on his door that spelled out STN, there was the sudden unmistakable howl of Roger Daltrey, followed by Stan's howl: "Won't get fooled again!"

Every neighborhood has its unofficial mayor: the old Japanese painter who sits on his front porch and chats it up; the retired black gentleman who sweeps his walk and smokes cigars; the Irishman who always magically appears whenever you need to slide into a slip and tie up your home. What we all need is a mayor who's rocking out to the Who.

The members of River Rats & Other Rodents are what you might expect of a crew who choose to live on boats in subzero temperatures. They're hardy, adventurous, kind people who will help you out when you need it but don't get involved in other people's business and expect you to stay out of theirs. When anything happens in the ma-

rina—a new boat coming in, a broken pumpout, a listing boat—
they come out in full force. Mark is never more excited than on a
Saturday morning when he rushes into the cabin where I am still
sleeping and starts hauling out tools. "Don's pipes burst in the bow
and we gotta help him," he says on the way out, trailing nuts and
bolts behind him. If you live on a boat, you need to know how to fix
things—often. And since nobody knows how to fix everything, you
need your neighbors to help. Five guys standing around trying to di-
agnose a stuttering generator is somehow better than just one. At
least you know somebody will have the right tool once you figure
out the problem.

While the camaraderie and technical help and occasional im-
promptu Sunday barbecues would seem to be the priorities of the association, River Rats & Other Rodents had one primary purpose: to
hold its annual holiday party.

Everyone decorated their boats with lights, hung mistletoe, put up a little tree, and lined the dock with towels so that in an ice storm, tipsy guests wouldn't go tipping over into the drink. They hopped from boat to boat, and ended the evening aboard *Venture On*, a two-story trawler captained by a charming, generous dentist. "This beam is heavenly," more than one guest commented, lounging in the living area that spanned eighteen feet across. It was so expansive you wouldn't know it was a boat, except for the occasional rocking in another boat's wake. By midnight, most of the invited guests had gone home, and the River Rats & Other Rodents donned their special hats (black trucker hats with rubber rodents glued to the bills) and commenced the annual business meeting, using Robert's Rules. A typical meeting began:

"I move that we all have a second drink before commencing the meeting."

"Any seconds?"

"I second."

"All in favor?"

All hands raise.

The annual meeting included elections of officers (primary role of the president is to plan the next holiday party; primary role of the vice president is to make sure everyone takes down their holiday decorations by Easter) and the awarding of the annual River Rat Bonehead Award.

Mark was the proud recipient of the Bonehead Award his first year in River City.

It happened about month into his ownership, a year before he met me, when it was time to pump out the sewage holding tank for the first time. It was autumn, and in the dark after work, he had trouble hooking up the marina's sewage hose to the sewage port aboard *Mazurka*. "It's a male fitting, and the pumpout has a female fitting that you connect to it. I couldn't figure out why it wasn't screwing in right. So I just forced it in." Of course, right? "I started pumping out. I noticed that there wasn't much coming out, so I figured it must be empty." He let the pump work for a while to make sure the tank was empty, then undid the hose.

Then he took his mom's advice and poured a cup of bleach down into the holding tank to keep it fresh. He closed the valve, cleaned up, went to bed. No problem.

"Except when I woke up in the morning, I realized that I pumped out my fuel tank and dumped in a cup of bleach."

Trying to pump out a fuel tank is not really a problem—the tank isn't set up to accommodate a pumpout, so nothing will pump out. But pouring bleach into the fuel tank is a whole 'nother story.

The previous owner had installed a fuel polisher that would clean fuel (like you might need in a foreign port). So Mark turned on the fuel polisher, hoping to clean the fuel of the bleach. He figured he should let it run for a while, since the fuel tanks were almost full. He left for work.

"That was my other mistake."

At work on the hospital unit, he received a page from River City reporting an oil slick behind his boat, and that they had received a call from the City of Chicago.

Mark panicked and raced to *Mazurka*.

"I was thinking about the fuel polisher and maybe something had sprung a leak and was pumping all the fuel into the river. I have a bilge pump, and if the bilge filled up, it might be pumping out through the bilge."

But on board, there was no fuel in the bilge, the area just below the engine in the bottom of the boat. Mark noticed there was fuel coming out of the sides of the boat. He got in his dinghy and paddled around the boat, trying to find the leak. The charming, generous *Venture On* captain came by and told him to get out of the water before he looked suspicious.

The fuel polisher and the bleach had started foaming the tank and seeping through the breather, creating an oil slick. Mark shut off the polisher and started wiping down the boat. It took a while for the fuel to stop foaming. Conveniently, he had already set up the de-icer, a powerful fan that suspends under the boat to keep the water circulating during winter and prevents ice from forming. He turned on the de-icer, and it began pushing the fuel away from his boat, toward *Venture On.* Adapt, overcome, improvise.

Just as he was cleaning up, he noticed the Chicago Police boat coming down the river toward him. He did what any captain would do—he ducked and hid. Peeking out the window, he thought of the ten-thousand-dollar fine for dumping fuel in the water. He thought about the EPA, lawyers' fees, jail, and the inevitable *Tribune* front-page story.

"The police came up. They kept going. They didn't see anything."

That December, the River Rats & Other Rodents awarded Mark the Bonehead Award, and he proudly donned the white plastic bone that fit over his head. And then the association elected him president.

OFF THE WALL

Mark lived under the radar. The oldest of nine children, he learned early to follow the rules just enough to keep everyone out of his business, but under the radar he did things his own way. Maybe it's the yooper ideal to do things your own way and buck the system? This is, after all, the appendage to Michigan that once lobbied to become the fifty-first state. (The state's name? The Superior State, of course.) When Mark was a kid, his under-the-radar skills got him out of ever washing a dish, folding laundry, or changing a diaper in a family of nine kids—and no one noticed.

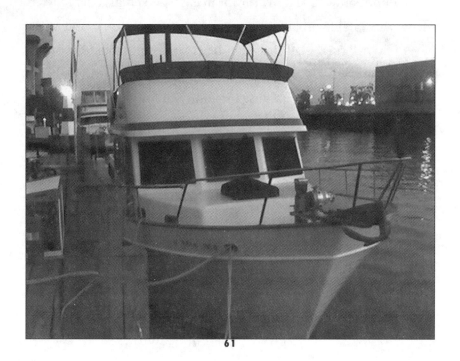

"I always felt like I didn't want to be like everyone else," he says. "There was some loneliness associated in not being like everyone else, but I thought I'd put up with the loneliness rather than conform."

I was not so much an under-the-radar kind of gal as I was a tagger-along of under-the-radar men. On the surface, I lived a fairly normal life, but I have a fondness for the unusual: spending six weeks in Russia with a ragtag group of writers, for instance, or interviewing the Chicago White Sox the year they won the pennant when I had almost no journalistic training, no knowledge of baseball, and absolutely no idea what I was doing.

I liked how Mark brought me into his under-the-radar business, like sneaking me into the River City parking garage for free, until one night when I drove too fast through the gate and it crashed down on his motorcycle, as he rode in behind me, necessitating a trip to Mohammed the Parking Man, an apology, a tip, and money for the gate repair.

Mark not only parked my car for free, he parked his boat for free. He was a veritable urban squatter, tied up to the outside wall of the River City Marina. Had the water been land, this would have been some of the priciest real estate in the city, with its unobstructed view of the Sears Tower, and its close proximity to Printers' Row, and the only thing standing between him and the Loop being the remarkable plot of unmowed, untended grass, the last piece of undeveloped land in all of gentrification-crazy, overdeveloped Chicago, a wild square where South Loopers let their dogs run free in the early evenings. Had the space where Mark squatted been solid, it would have been worth thousands in tax revenue. But it wasn't land. He was sitting right over an abandoned marina gas pump on the one body of water Chicago has never had much respect for, the "second" body of water, if you will, the river at the heart of it all.

Of the books cramming Mark's scant shelves, Libby Hill's *The Chicago River: A Natural and Unnatural History* stood alone as *Mazurka*'s personal guidebook, the phone book for her neighborhood, a tome singing the praises of a river that has been abused, mistreated, and misunderstood, always sliding along under the radar, much like a liveaboard. Mark met the author just a few months after he had moved aboard. "Best wishes for life on the river!" she inscribed on the inside cover. Published in 2000, it is the first and only comprehensive biography of a river that shaped Chicago as much as Chicago shaped it. The story of the Chicago River, Hill writes, is a "microcosm of the uneasy relation between nature and civilization, especially when the welfare of a great city is at stake."

The Chicago River once lay beneath calm tropical seas. A glacier came and receded, followed by people—big-game hunters, and then Archaic, Woodland, and Mississippian cultures, and then Jean Baptiste Point du Sable, who built a farm on the northern bank at the mouth of the river in the late eighteenth century, and then more of his kind, who established Fort Dearborn on the opposite bank in 1808, right where the Michigan Avenue Bridge stands today.

In the early nineteenth century, the river was regarded as not much more than a lazy, sluggish creek that opened into Lake Michigan, interrupted by a sandbar. Settlers at Fort Dearborn began digging to alter the drainage pattern almost immediately, as well as dumping sewage and even alcohol (to keep the native population from taking their supply). The white people's descent transformed the river into a sewer. Chicago grew, more people arrived from all over the world, more people to dump their sewage and garbage into the river, which naturally flowed into Lake Michigan, the clean water source for the city. Chicagoans called it the Stinking River. The south fork of the Main Stem, which served as the sewer for the union stockyards and meatpacking industry, was known as "Bubbly Creek."

In 1900, in a feat of modern civil engineering, the Sanitary District of Chicago reversed the flow of the river using a series of canal locks, forcing the river to flow into the newly completed Chicago Sanitary and Ship Canal.

Chicago's garbage would now flow south, toward the Mississippi River basin.

With my small worldview of the vastness of rivers, where rivers flood even though you try to dam them up, I find it impossible to fathom the extent to which Chicago has manipulated and cajoled this once sluggish creek into doing precisely what the city wants it to do. A little digging here, a little straightening there, move this piece, open that arm, dredge here and fill in the gap there, and suddenly we have a river that's going to do exactly what we want it to do, exactly when we want it to do it, no questions asked.

Daniel Burnham envisioned the river in his 1909 *Plan of Chicago* as a centerpiece of beauty in Chicago. The city was changing its attitude toward its water. As Hill puts it, "The evolving science of ecology, the growing sophistication concerning public health and cleanliness, and the emerging ideal of civic beauty impacted the idea of river improvements."

With the advent of the twentieth century and the opening of the Sanitary and Ship Canal, water from Lake Michigan mixed with river water, making it clean enough to swim. From 1908 to 1930, the Chicago River Marathon took swimmers three miles, from the east end of the Main Stem to Jackson Boulevard. Cruise ships carried tourists. In the summer of 1915, twenty-five hundred passengers boarded the *Eastland*, a steamer bound for the Western Electric Company picnic in Michigan City, Indiana. Overloaded with passengers, the ship broke free and rolled just a few feet from shore, killing more than eight hundred people.

Though Chicagoans couldn't escape their garbage for long. The river still hobbled under the weight of its pollution. "Friends of the River" organized, and with other groups and the cooperation of a mayor who valued the city parks and waterways, a massive river cleaning effort gained momentum in the 1990s. The fish population—largemouth and smallmouth bass, crappie, bluegill, catfish, and carp—rebounded. In one of his famous off-the-cuff statements, Mayor Daley pronounced in July 2007 that he would even eat fish caught in the river. So the *Chicago Sun-Times* (whose office is right on the river) sent its outdoors columnist Dale Bowman with a fishing rod out to the Orleans Bridge. Bowman caught bluegill, pumpkinseed, and rock bass and sent them to a lab to be tested for mercury and other toxins, including PCBs (polychlorinated biphenyls). The Illinois Environmental Protection Agency said they were safe—but for no more than one 8-ounce meal per month.

I always thought the river was too polluted to hold any fish, until one night as I walked out to *Mazurka* there came the unmistakable sound of a flopping splash beneath my feet. "I'm going to catch that fish," Mark said, "I'm going to catch him and eat him."

Soon it was too cold to go out on the lake, and we stayed on the river. Winter was approaching.

Distracted by his new girlfriend, Mark procrastinated and put off the work necessary to prepare his boat to endure Chicago's long winter. I didn't even know there was any work to be done until an unexpected snowstorm in early December dumped half a foot of snow on us, inspiring Mark to pull an all-night shrink-wrap session. He didn't invite me along. I had no idea what he was preparing to do, but he was definitely intent on the task ahead. I stayed at my apartment that night, sleeping soundly in my own bed; when next I saw *Mazurka*, she was gift-wrapped for the holidays in white plastic from bow to stern. Only her windows remained uncovered. "I'm not living in an igloo," Mark declared.

The boat needed whatever natural light she could get. Winter hours of sunlight are slight in the cavern of the South Loop. Sky-scrapers squash the sun's low arc, and our ball of light and warmth hardly peeks over the condos of River City before descending too quickly behind the post office and its chunks of concrete and steel.

One gray January morning Mark came out on dock and found a note taped to his shrink wrap. It was signed by a guy with the same last name as the infamous cow owner, representing the River City condo association, asking Mark to call him.

This did not bode well; *Mazurka* had made a blip on someone's radar.

Mr. Cow Owner was friendly yet direct on the phone. It was illegal to moor a boat in that spot. Mark would have to move into one of the marina slips or else the condo association would call the police and have him towed.

River City wanted him off the wall.

In a city full of under-the-radar politics, River City fits right in. In all the time we spent in the marina, we never really knew who was running the show—the property management company? The condo association? The building itself is confusing: a Jetson mini city built by Bertrand Goldberg, the designer of the Marina Towers, cartoonish in its roundness, its first-floor physician offices, stores, and gym, its oddly shaped units with bubble windows, and its atrium rising from the fifth floor to the roof. You can pay for a fantastic view of downtown or a terrible view of other buildings. It's one of the only condos in the city with a marina, and units sold with the idea that you could park your boat in your backyard. Mark had considered one of the units in his real estate hunt, in fact, but decided he would rather just live in the backyard.

And now not only did he like that spot on the wall, but his boat was wrapped in plastic.

Mark delayed matters. He begged more time to find a slip. He called around town; the Coast Guard said it was not illegal to park there, as did Chicago Police. The space wasn't technically owned by River City, since it was on the outside wall, so he wasn't officially trespassing, though to be fair, *Mazurka* did benefit from River City's electricity, water, and pumpout. Mark tried to reason with Mr. Cow Owner that it was winter, his boat was wrapped in plastic—how was he going to move it even if he could find a slip? The condo association was unsympathetic; the boat had to go. Was it a matter of trespassing, or river regulation, or condo association politics? The reasons were vague, though it was clear that Mr. Cow Owner would have no problem towing the boat, and there would be nothing vague about coming home to find your home gone.

Oh, Cap Streeter, where were you when we needed you?

On a bitter-cold January morning, the River Rats and a few brave friends came out in down jackets and thick gloves, carrying long gaff poles, hooks, and lines. Carefully, they massaged, maneuvered, and coaxed the gift-wrapped *Mazurka* away from the wall, across the opening of the marina, and into a slip just inside the wall on the south side. Mark now had a lease and paid rent to the slip owner; he was legitimate. His view of the Sears Tower remained the same, his view of the river obscured by *Venture On*. Here *Mazurka* rested for the remainder of the snowless winter. After the freak snowstorm in December, it never snowed again.

Sometimes that winter, when I was walking on the dock, I would watch the river and its swirls like eddies, and I would forget which way the marvels of engineering had forced it to flow. At times, it would appear as if it was flowing out toward Lake Michigan.

Engineers also noticed this phenomenon. In January 1998, scientists from the U.S. Geological Survey, taking routine measurements in the Chicago River, noticed something unexpected: Measurements taken at the Columbus Drive bridge had recorded a bi-directional flow in the river. At the surface, water was flowing away from Lake Michigan, the way people intended. Below, near the riverbed, water was traveling toward the lake, the way nature intended.

Researchers at the University of Illinois in Urbana built a simulation of the Chicago River and proved that density currents were responsible for the bi-directional flow. Water density can be influenced by temperature, and when water of different densities mixes, it can create density currents. The water at the surface was less dense than the water near the riverbed. "A river under a river," lead researcher Professor Marcelo García called it.

During the summer, when river traffic and the water temperature are high, the river flows the way we want it to go. But in the winter, it resumes its normal path, even if only far below the surface.

In this huge metropolis, after almost two centuries of being told where to go and how, the river is quietly bucking the Man, moving the way it wants to go—under the radar.

MY FIRST GOOSE

Spring comes slowly to Chicago. The March air hangs heavy and damp for far too long, mounting many gray mornings with a clammy cold that works its way under your skin, worse than any January snowstorm. It can be a depressing time, especially if you're feeling entitled to something good and warm and filled with sunshine.

Being in love helps. By early spring, Mark and I were firmly entrenched in our romance. We hiked in Yosemite; we spent Christmas with my brother's family in California. I was spending more and more time at *Mazurka*, even when Mark was away on business. I would sit in the salon and try to feel him in the space around me. I'd read his magazines, look out the window, drink up his wine and whiskey. I had begun to feel an anxious longing I wasn't ready to talk about. I knew I was in love with Mark. I knew he was in love with me. The relationship was clearly growing. But toward what? My divorce was finalized in January (with no kids, no assets, and no property, things move pretty fast). Now I was free, really single—and where were we heading?

Love, let's be honest, is painful in the beginning. Exhilarating, yes, but full of anxiety and anticipation. The heart is opening, but the opening can be laborious. And once it's opened, then what? The whole world is turned upside down, and we must recalibrate. It takes time. It takes time, first, to figure out what's going on inside, and

then time to reconcile the inside with the outside world. The discomfort lies in the friction between the way we used to be, and the way we are just yet becoming. And that's just within us—isn't there another person involved here? Who can guess what they're feeling.

Mark says he never felt any of this drama. Falling in love with me was calm, constant—his feelings for me remained steady and consistent, and he just knew.

Long before the city registered that winter's respite was on its way, the one telltale sign of spring appeared: Our early mornings were pierced by the unmistakable honking of Canada geese.

In the last part of the nineteenth century, when Chicago was having a field day dumping its garbage into the river, early North American settlers were also having a field day hunting Canada geese, and the fowl almost completely disappeared from southern Canada and the northern United States. In the early 1900s, when Chicagoans started cleaning up their river, Canada geese began their comeback. Birds from captive breeding flocks were reintroduced to their natural habitat. By 1950, there were an estimated one million Canada geese in North America; fifty years later, there were more than eight million.

Maybe I exaggerate, but it seems half that population explosion, like their human counterparts, had settled in Chicago and its suburbs. The geese, like people, value the neatly mowed lawns and the fake fountains and ponds surrounding corporate campuses. They love golf courses that provide plenty of flat area to graze and help them easily spot predators. They like fertilized turf grass for the tender shoots, a staple in their diet. Ponds give them safe escape and a place to sleep at night. A fountain keeps the water moving in the winter, creating a year-round home for these geese. In northeastern Illinois, there are two types of Canada geese (of the eleven races); those who migrate, and those who stay around all year. They all produce poop. Studies at Cornell University have shown that a goose can transform food into waste in seven minutes, and in a day a Canada goose produces a pound of poop. Multiply that by eighty-six thousand (the actual number of Canada geese estimated in northeast Illinois in 2001), and you've got eighty-six thousand pounds of new poop covering the Chicago area each day.

Mark and I learned to sidestep the many land mines of green poop covering the dock and long cement walkway connecting the marina to the parking area. The walkway rose six feet out of the water and extended from the marina along a narrow grassy riverbank. About fifty yards south of *Mazurka* stood a large planter, four feet high, ten feet in diameter. In the summer, this planter was filled with red geraniums; in the early spring, it displayed a short tree surrounded by shrubs and some weeds and dirt. With the arrival of Canada geese, we would be greeted each morning as we passed the planter by four or five geese hanging out in front, like neighborhood guys sitting on a stoop. As we passed, the largest one—the one around whom the others seemed to be gathered—would open his black beak, stick out his tongue, and hiss at us. It was funny, and a little freaky. I hissed back.

At the lakefront, I had run through gaggles of geese often enough, and they dispersed in a friendly, non-aggressive manner, as per their evolutionary understanding that I, as the human runner, was atop the food chain, and they, as fowl with brains the size of a peanut, would do best to look out.

That spring, Mark went away for nearly two weeks, first to Canada to climb frozen waterfalls with Scott, then to south Texas, to visit his parents at their winter home. While he was gone I lolled around, keeping busy, counting days. I stayed away from *Mazurka*, finding it too lonely there without him. Finally, on the last Sunday in March, I picked him up in the evening from Midway airport. We swung by the post office to collect a huge pile of mail and headed to River City. As we made our way down the walkway, we came upon the planter and there, in a brand-new nest under the tree, sat a goose.

Spring had come! The geese were nesting! Soon there would be warm days, sunshine, new life!

Mark led the way, pulling his suitcase behind him, its wheels clicking over the gaps between the dock's wood planks. Cell phone to his ear, he was telling his mom that he had arrived safely. I followed, carrying the massive pile of mail. As we rounded the bend, nearing the nest built about chest height, we met another goose—presumably her mate—waddling toward us from the other side. He was hissing.

Mark took a big step toward it, aggressively. The goose flew off, into the water, and we continued around the planter.

But then something unexpected happened. Something that set a new tone to the warmth and kind anticipation of a gentle spring.

Behind us, the male goose only grazed the water; just as his webbed feet hit the surface, he took off again into the air, swooped around, and came after us. These giant Canada geese (yes, the official term for this race is *giant*) can weigh up to seventeen pounds and have a wingspan of more than six feet, and one was coming down on me fast. I covered my head with the stack of mail and made a run for the boat, passing Mark with his suitcase and phone call. I could hear the wings flapping behind me, and then he was down upon me, the gross and terrifying weight of his large, feathered round body resting upon my head for just a moment before he soared off. He didn't have time for another pass before we were out of his territory, but we kept running, laughing in fear, Mark telling his mom, "We've just been attacked by a goose!"

Family bonds among Canada geese are strong. They mate for life, which can be anywhere from ten to twenty-four years (though if one mate dies, the widow will remarry), and goslings begin communicating with their parents while still in the egg, giving out little peeps or high-pitched trills to show contentment, like a cat purring. Once out of the egg, goslings stay with their parents for up to a year; when you look up in the sky to a V of honking, migrating Canada geese, it's actually a caravan of families traveling together. Each spring, they return to the same spot where they've had reproductive success in the past to lay a new clutch of eggs. Sort of like humans return to their honeymoon spots years later.

We like the place where love lies—we think it brings us luck.

Thus began a new ritual for *Mazurka*, the daily dance of approaching or leaving the boat. When we neared the nest, the wife would sit firmly still while her husband would come waddling around, attacking us on land, or swoop down into the water, curve back, and come at us from the air. Mark didn't mind the goose so much—he would brace himself, pretend to charge him, and stride by. But there were times when fear immobilized my feet and I couldn't make the pass. One Saturday afternoon as we returned from shopping downtown, Mark went ahead, but I could not move. I stayed by the parking lot while Mark headed toward the nest. On cue, the goose rounded the planter, waddling straight for him; I shuddered, unable to watch. But Mark had the right idea and charged ahead, so that the goose, despite his hissing and ruffling feathers, had no choice but to fly into the water, lest he be run over. After Mark passed through, the goose returned to his post, watching me. I sat down on the ledge near the parking lot, trying to look casual. I studied the goose, attempting to figure him out. Can you reason with a goose? Do they learn? After a while, would he grow used to us? Could we win him over with food? What does a goose eat, anyway? Mark called me on my cell phone, and though I hated being the scaredy-cat girlfriend, he returned like the ferryman Charon, taking me over the River Styx. The goose stayed clear of us.

What I really wanted to know was how long it would take those eggs to cook and hatch so the geese would leave and I could resume my own happy courtship. This goose's family life was taking a serious toll on my own attempts at mating. The answer? Twenty-five to thirty days. If I avoided *Mazurka*, which I was doing more often these days, I would miss spring on the river—the opening of leaves, the sailboats floating along on newly warm afternoons. I told my friend Kathy at lunch, "I think the geese are going to keep me from seeing my boyfriend for the next month!"

"Oh, they're nasty bastards," she said, relating a story of her great-grandmother in Poland, attacked by a goose who clamped down on her leg at a family picnic. She had to bash it against a tree before it would let go. Luckily, Great-Grandmother survived with only a few stitches. The goose was probably not as fortunate.

Mark told the River Rats about his problems with attack geese. They related the story of another liveaboard who stayed in the same slip where *Mazurka* presently moored. He was a heavy drinker and would wake in a foul mood when the geese started honking early in the morning. One day he had enough; he came out and opened fire. Shot one goose and killed it. The Chicago Police came out, and the Environmental Protection Agency, and they fined him and barred him from the river for life.

Short of gunfire, we looked for other deterrents: plastic or live swans (which people say don't work), fake alligators for ponds (also said not to work), bright streamers, flags, balloons (whose color and flapping-in-the-wind noise is supposed to annoy geese), and my favorite—specially trained dogs.

Some areas use border collies in the morning and afternoon during migration to clear away the geese. If a flock of geese flying over what looks to be a great area sees it's empty of their kind, they'll think there's a reason why and move on. There's even a story about a blind and deaf great horned owl who successfully scared away two flocks of geese from the Winnipeg Airport property just by hooting.

From late June to late July, geese molt, losing their flight feathers and the ability to fly. Because they're defenseless during the molting season, city governments have been known to use this time to round up geese and kill them. After slaughter, some places will distribute the meat to food pantries. There's even a website, Canada Goose Hall of Shame, which lists shameless cities participating in this massacre, including Milwaukee, St. Louis, and Sault Sainte Marie, Michigan.

A method of goose reproduction control that is often endorsed by animal rights organization as a humane alternative to slaughter and gassing is called egg addling, in which the nest is interrupted, and the eggs are shaken (by humans) and coated with corn oil. Geese do not know the goslings in their eggs have been destroyed and they continue incubation. GeesePeace, the Canadian Wildlife Service, and the U.S. Fish and Wildlife Service all use this practice.

After watching Mama Goose sit on her nest all day and all night, through wind and sleet, icy rain, and steaming-hot sunny afternoons, hardly leaving her post for a month, this method seems the cruelest torture of all. What agony to sit for over a month straight on a carefully tended nest, only to see that all your efforts are in vain, and once again you are without offspring.

I thought of the women I knew who were jumping through hoops just to get that one egg fertilized. . . .

And besides, these geese wouldn't realize their eggs were defunct until the end of the season. They would still spend a month sitting out there, attacking us. I didn't want to decrease the goose population—I just wanted to walk to my boyfriend's house without being attacked.

I called my dad to get his advice. "They're not that far above fish," he suggested. "If it comes after you, just snap its neck." I imagined crossing the dock, the goose attaching itself to my arm, and me reaching around to grab its neck and kill it. I would have my first goose.

"My First Goose" is Isaac Babel's terrifically dense short story about a bespectacled soldier, a graduate of St. Petersburg Law, sent to the Cossacks during the revolution. He is advised by the quartermaster to earn the respect of his comrades by messing up a lady, "and a good lady, too." Instead, he kills a goose in a scene as violating as any rape, and gives it to the landlady to cook, the landlady who says twice that with everything going on she wants to hang herself. The story ends with the bespectacled soldier reading *Pravda* to his new colleagues, around a campfire, "spying out exultingly the secret curve of Lenin's straight line," and then going to sleep and dreaming of women. "But my heart, stained with bloodshed, grated and brimmed over."

Rather than carry the guilt of my first goose, I started carrying an umbrella.

With the flimsy shield for protection, I could pass by unaided, bracing myself as I neared the nest. I learned it was important not to startle the husband, so I would make gruff stomping noises as I approached. It was best not to look him in the eye, not to acknowledge his presence at all, and never, ever, to look at his wife, sitting atop the nest. The goose was always on duty, and often would dive-bomb me; I raised my umbrella above my head, keeping him at a clear distance, his weight slowly shredding the poor nylon. Some nights, when he must have been exhausted from a day spent battling foes, he would only hiss meanly and let me pass.

One night when I skittered by the nest without much turmoil, I arrived at *Mazurka* and while standing in the salon, casually looked out the window toward the river. There was the goose, circling in the current, watching me. I ventured out on the dock and stood tall; he circled closer. We stared each other down, the river's reflection of the Sears Tower lighting our showdown. In the quiet pulse of the central post office's late-night business, the quiet din of sleeping factories, the towers overlooking us, this was an ancient standoff, irrelevant of the massive city of shoulders enclosing us—this was man against beast.

Then in the first warm week of spring, mid-April, Daddy Goose calmed down. Mark reasoned we were getting close to hatching time. One afternoon the nest was surprisingly unguarded; I hovered a moment, then noticed the pair coming down the river. The next weekend, the manic goose and his wife were gone, their nest filled with eggshells. We never saw them hatch, never saw the goslings, never saw them go. We spent a month under attack and never got to see the cute little babies.

Mark and I resumed normal life, still instinctively bracing ourselves as we passed by the first nest, two humans trained by geese to have a Pavlovian response to crossing their territory.

And one morning, as we wove through parents dropping off their kids at River City day care, we looked over to the opposite side of the harbor. There, on the grassy bluff beside the river, half a dozen geese wandered around. Among their webbed feet twittered a gaggle of little goslings. One by one the adult geese approached the edge and dropped into the river, until only the goslings were left on shore, restless and jittering without their parents. Then they got the idea; in single file, they dropped down into the river with little plops, and once they had all landed in the river they started to swim behind their mother upstream, with Daddy following close behind.

SOUTH HOTEL TEN

When everything in life is changing, when everything is new and there is no status quo, no "normal" anymore, it's easy to lose context for standard behavior. Everything is relative, after all. An event that would have been insane five years ago suddenly seems par for the course. Falling in love is crazy; falling in love with a man who lives on a boat is bizarre; when, after nine months of dating, he says he's moving his home out to a mooring can on Lake Michigan for the summer, somehow, oddly enough, this seems normal.

If you've ever seen a landscape photo of Chicago in summertime, chances are it included Monroe Harbor. Along the lakefront bordering the long green space of downtown Grant Park, Buckingham Fountain sprays in the distance, and hundreds of sailboats sit calmly atop the glassy lake, as if tied to nothing. In fact, they are tied to an individual mooring can, a white dome that looks like a buoy and is anchored to the lake floor. Using a split line, the boat is tethered to the can, completely surrounded by water. There are about a thousand mooring cans in Monroe Harbor.

It can be tough to get a slip in the Chicago harbors, especially in the harbors on the popular North Side, which are easier for large boats to get into and have docks. To climb the harbor ladder to a dock, most boaters pay their dues by spending a summer on a can. The previous summer when I met him, Mark had a spot in Monroe

Harbor, but, anxious about swinging around a can all summer, stayed at River City for the season, paying rent on two spots. So the following year, bolstered by machismo or economics, he decided to try out the can at South Hotel Ten.

Like Chicago, Monroe Harbor is divided into a north side and south side, and like Chicago the north end is for the rich with the more expensive, impatient boats, and the south for those of us who just slipped in under the wire. Each side has rows designated by letters, and for clarity, boaters use the phonetic alphabet: alpha-bravo-charlie-delta-echo-foxtrot-golf-hotel-india-juliet-kilo-lima-mike-november-oscar-papa-quebec-romeo-sierra-tango-uniform-victor-whiskey-xray-yankee-zulu. In each row, the cans are numbered, so like the city every boat in the harbor has its address by direction, street, and house number. The north side is generally calmer, while the south siders get whipped around by the northeastern winds and rollers coming into the harbor. And like Chicago el riders, boaters in Monroe Harbor, whether north siders or south siders, all rely on the same mode of public transportation: the tender boats.

These blue taxi boats, holding just a couple on a lonely Tuesday morning, or crammed with twenty or thirty passengers on a busy Saturday afternoon, shuttle boaters back and forth to their individual cans from 9 a.m. until 11 p.m. on weekdays, and twenty-four hours a day on weekends. Boaters are given a couple of season passes to ride the tender boats, and their visitors can buy tickets at the harbor window. At the harbor office dock, people line up, waiting to board the taxis. When boaters are ready to come in from their day on the water, they switch their radios to Channel 68, listen for a moment to make sure it's clear, then call, "Monroe Harbor, this is South Hotel Ten, requesting a pickup for two. Over." The airwaves are filled with the poetry of the harbor addresses: *North Charlie Sixteen, South Whiskey Twelve, North Echo Ten*. Though I can't say for sure, I'd guess my favorite Chicago band got its album name—*Yankee Hotel Foxtrot*—from the Chicago harbors. "I hear all you singing out there," Jeff Tweedy called to his devoted fans one beautiful summer evening from the stage at Millennium Park. "And who's going to stop you? The Chicago skyline? I don't think so."

The licensed tender captains were a motley crew with stories more interesting than their passengers. One had long white hair, a silent, Australian-bouncer looking guy. Another was short and squat, a retired DEA cop who married his sweetheart, his former housecleaner. There was the hippie who just moved back from a quarter century living in Manhattan, returning to the Midwest and living on her sailboat in the harbor. One snacked on edamame throughout his shift, tossing the soybean shells in the lake. In all, there were maybe a dozen tender boat drivers, and over that summer we got to know all of them in bits and pieces, short conversations while they sidled up beside each boat and helped folks clamor off, carrying coolers and kids, bags of groceries and ice, and lots and lots of beer. For Mark, they were more than just water taxi drivers; they were the doormen to his floating home, the watchmen who kept tabs on *Mazurka* when he was away. They knew Mark was a liveaboard; they saw him every day; and for this reason, they gave him special attention and a little extra respect. He was not a drunk weekender with a bad sunburn and a mouthy disposition. He was out there day in and day out, battling four-foot waves and a sporadic generator. He was in this for real.

And there is nothing more real for a boater than living on a mooring can. (Though winter might give a can a run for its money.) When your boat is tethered to a can, the simplest things take on a new challenge. You cannot walk out to your boat; you take the tender. And if the tender service is not working, you row your own boat. You not only row your boat, but you row anything you might be carrying with you: groceries, laundry, engine oil. When you get to your boat, you must haul everything up to the deck and tie up your dinghy. Because you have no dock, you also have no electricity hookup, which means when you arrive home, you must run your generator if you want to plug in your phone, your laptop, your lamp. (The refrigerator, engine batteries, and some lights run on a second power source that is always on.) Without electricity, there is nothing to run the hot-water heater (so if you are looking to take a hot shower after work, you'd best do it at the gym, unless you want to wait an hour for those precious six gallons). You must make a special trip to the dock to fill your water tanks and empty your sewage. And when the wind is up and the waves are high, so are you.

Shortly after Mark moved *Mazurka* out to South Hotel Ten (and spent more than a few nights at the solid-ground living of my Bucktown apartment), we flew to Anchorage, Alaska, so he could interview for a job. I loved the idea of moving to Alaska and declared I would move with him if he got the position. After the interview, we drove to Seward and hired a fishing charter for a day, then completed a five-day backpacking trek to Hope, via forty miles of the Resurrection Pass.

On the morning of our departure, while loading up our backpacks at a picnic table along the Russian River campground, I heard a rustling in the woods. I looked up to see a big brown bear, wide as a picnic table, rumbling toward me, roly-poly on all four legs. I screamed and ran for the car, leaving Mark standing there, "What? What?" looking for his camera. Luckily, the bear veered to the left, but this set the stage for our backpacking adventure (especially when

I later heard that the year prior, someone in the campground had been killed by a brown bear). With bear bells ringing and bear Mace at the ready, I followed Mark into the Resurrection Pass.

On our first night, at a campsite where our food was safely stored in the bear box and Mark was pitching our tent fifty yards away, I was looking through his pack for something when I came across a small white bag with a red bow on it. It was about the size of a ring box. I tucked it away quickly. *This is it.* Sometime during this trip, he was going to ask me. I could barely contain myself.

As we finished our dinner around the fire, the early Alaskan summer wilderness surrounding us with its limitless light, Mark handed me the box. Inside, the simple white gold band had seven small diamonds across it. It didn't look like I thought an engagement ring should look (I never had one the first time around). He did not get down on one knee. He did not ask, "Will you marry me?" Instead, Mark said, "I appreciate that you are willing to come to Alaska with me if I get this job. I want to show my commitment to you, too."

I paused. "You mean this is a promise ring?"

"Yeah, I guess so."

Sarcasm was my response to disappointment. "Are you going to give me your letterman jacket, too?"

He didn't get the joke.

So here we have our first lesson in connotations and semantics. The word: *commitment*. Mark's understanding: She's willing to come to Alaska with me, and I'm not going to bail on her when she gets here. My understanding: We're getting married. I had too many expectations of this relationship to just let things rest at a "commitment." By the time we hiked out of the Alaskan wilderness four days later, I had it all planned. Mark would get the job; we would get married that summer in Chicago; by fall, we'd be living in Anchorage as husband and wife. The day we flew out of Anchorage, we toured some houses. On land.

We returned to Chicago and began preparations to leave. Anticipating that the job offer would come by June or July, we needed to plan the wedding quickly. We met with Father Jerry at Holy Family parish on Roosevelt Road—the second oldest Catholic Church in Chicago—and set a date for the end of September.

Holy Family was unlike any Catholic church I ever knew. In fact, the community inside its doors brought me back to the Catholic faith. I went with Mark early in our dating, because he convinced me it was unusual. First of all, there was the music—a gospel choir led by Sam Parker, filled with people of every race with incredible voices. And then there was the pause about halfway through the service, when Father Jerry announced, "Let us offer one another a sign of the Lord's peace." Everyone did what I had learned to expect from my childhood—they turned first to the families, shaking hands, kissing, then to those in the pew in front of them, then to those behind. And then, when I assumed we'd get on with the rest of the show, the parishioners did something I'd never seen before: They left their pews. They began walking the aisles, shaking hands and offering peace to every person they saw: young, old, black, white, Latino, Asian. The banner at the altar proclaimed, HOLY FAMILY: OUR DOORS ARE OPEN WIDE, and indeed, everybody was welcome, everybody part of the family.

It was at this church that I returned to the sacrament of Reconciliation. I was alone at Mass one Sunday during Lent (Mark was out of town—and I went anyway) when they offered the sacrament during the service. Priests stood around the perimeter, and people lined up to talk with them. I sat watching for a long time. The need for reconciliation with a priest as intermediary was something I had long railed against. But finally I approached a priest whom I had never seen and would likely never see again. "I have problems with drinking and drugs," I whispered in his ear, my voice breaking. He said a blessing over me and I returned to the pew.

Shortly after, I quit doing both. No big deal.

No big deal until one night about a month later, I sat in a restaurant facing a wall full of booze, and I knew I would drink again— soon. "You gotta help me not start again," I told Mark. He agreed. But a few weeks later I was at a magazine release party in a bar (again, no big deal). At intermission I found myself standing at the bar. "Didn't you just read?" the cool chick bartender said. "Yes," I told her. "I really liked your story," she said. "Can I buy you a beer?" "Yes," I said, "Yes, you can." And I started drinking again—no big deal.

But the Sunday of my confession, sitting in the pew at Holy Family, I felt the rush of admitting I had a problem, and the relief that followed.

Holy Family was saved from the Great Chicago Fire in the nineteenth century, and saved from the wrecking ball in the twentieth. It became the first true congregation I ever felt a part of, and I was excited that we would be having a full Mass for our wedding.

At our interview with Father Jerry, he asked if either of us had been married before. I admitted I had, a civil ceremony in Vegas. I feared this meant I would have to go through a huge annulment process, that it would delay our marriage, or that we would not be able to get married at all.

"Different time, different place," Father Jerry said. I nodded. We moved on.

In a lot of ways, Holy Family embodied what I loved about Chicago. Everyone from every culture coming together for a single purpose—to worship in a church or to live in a city. We don't always get along, but in our best moments we are willing to put our hand out to anyone we meet, and our doors are open wide.

My mind obsessively brewed images of Alaska. What I thought would be my last summer in Chicago had become like a trip to the Art Institute, where I concentrated and imprinted the works of Monet and Renoir and Degas in my mind, so I could keep them with me forever. I wanted to memorize each sensory detail of the city: the smell of stagnant air when passing over a grate; black exhaust billowing from atop buses; the heavy, suffocating quilt of sound when standing on Wabash during rush hour, surrounded by cars and construction and an el train or two roaring overhead; the multicultural deep-fried frenzy of funnel cakes and southern chitlins at a summer neighborhood street festival; the feel of my pores opening during a long run at the lake on a hot, humid summer night, and the perfect timing of a rain shower in the last mile. I wanted to capture a perfect image of everything I saw: rows of condos along Lake Shore Drive; neighborhood tree-lined streets where Mexican and Japanese kids played together; sculptures erupting downtown, courthouses and banks built around them; church steeples and block-long community gardens; and people—people everywhere—nearly three million of us waiting in line at the grocery store and posted on corners selling drugs and riding bicycles to work and impatiently trying to get around tourists walking five abreast on Michigan Avenue. I wanted to remember this all because I had hated this city and learned to love this city and in a few short months it would no longer be mine.

Most of all, I wanted to imprint the unexpected moments when suddenly, for no explicable reason, everything suddenly stopped. These moments might happen at any time—during a New Year's blizzard or on a busy Saturday afternoon of errands and ball games or at the onset of a summer evening, in the shift from rush hour to recreation, sitting on the aft deck with the man who would be my husband. This was the moment I most wanted to preserve—a Chicago like Seurat's *A Sunday on the Isle of La Grande Jatte*: one moment of perfect stillness made up of millions of frantic, fast-moving points.

In late June, swinging around a can, Mark began work on a project from a long list of random someday to-do items (which included installing a movie screen on the aft deck and buying a projector so we could watch movies outside, marine drive-in style). When he said, "I really need to varnish the teak on the boat," I didn't pay much attention, nor did I comprehend what that meant—like what teak was, or how much time it would take, or how it would involve me.

Mazurka is an old boat, and one of its best features is its teak—the lovely, toffee-toned wood that makes up the railings surrounding the entire deck and the flybridge. And the trim around the windows and doors. And the doors themselves—three total, plus cupboard doors on the flybridge. And let's not forget that the entire interior is made of teak—though I thank God that in the summer of our engagement, Mark did not attempt to refinish the inside of the boat.

Once we washed away the bugs and spiderwebs and daily debris that accumulated on a boat, the first task was to strip all the old varnish using a soy-based gel paint stripper. Stripping must not be done too far in advance of the actual varnishing; leaving wood exposed for too long will damage it. It's not like you can strip the wood on a free weekend and then spend two months harbor-hopping before finishing the job. The work has to be in a tight time frame. Varnishing must be done on dry days, when there is no chance of rain for the next twenty-four hours, and preferably not in the hot sun. This weather combination is nearly impossible when you are tethered to a mooring can in downtown Chicago. Varnishing one coat, or even two, might be manageable— but the captain envisioned at least six coats of varnish. Physical labor was his way of dealing with change. *Slather, strip, sand, varnish, slather, strip, sand, varnish.* Slowly he worked his way through layers and layers of old varnish, to the raw wood underneath. He got rid of the old to make way for the new. While he worked, sailboats around us threw off their tethers and sailors waved, cruising off for cooler harbors. *Slather, strip, sand, varnish, repeat.* I was irritated that he would spend so much time on a project I didn't find interesting or necessary. Weren't we about to take off on the next great adventure? I liked hanging out on the boat, sure; I liked bringing my friends aboard for a fancy cruise along the shoreline. But spend blessed summer days varnishing? The work itself was not so difficult, but the moments of inactivity in between work could crush your soul; the weekends that passed in rainstorms, or blistering sun, or summer obligations of picnics and parties or wedding planning or out-of-town visitors. All the while, we waited. Waited for good weather, for free Saturdays, for the motivation and ambition to slather, strip, sand, varnish, repeat. Waited for word from Anchorage. Tethered to a mooring can, waiting.

By July, Alaska looked less likely. I struggled for patience, to live in the present. I started drinking again, casually. I avoided talking with Mark about what we were going to do if we had to stay in Chicago. None of it felt right or real. I did not want to be in Chicago past October; I was done with the city, done with my job, done with my apartment, done with life in the Lower Forty-Eight. I wanted adventure—I wanted to live in Alaska!

One thing for sure—I did *not* want to live on *Mazurka.*

Quaint as it was, the boat was smaller than my tiny one-bedroom apartment. Thirty-eight feet long, with a beam of 13 feet, the salon would serve as our living room and kitchen and had about 140 square feet of living space. The master stateroom had a queen-sized bed with two feet of walking space surrounding it. I always felt like I was scooting around Mark when we were inside. Where would I practice yoga? Where would I write? Carrying a backpack for weekends was only mildly inconvenient—but living full-time? Where would I hang my clothes, put my books? There was no full-length mirror, not even a real full-sized shower. And half a refrigerator? How would we cook meals? And what about Leo and Hunter, my two white, (very) long-haired cats?

Mark didn't know if he could live on land in Chicago. I couldn't blame him. He was unbelievably happy on his boat. The very reason he could stay in the city was because he figured out a way to live in nature. He'd grown up in miles and miles of northern woods on Lake Superior; he'd spent his twenties on a Navajo reservation in Arizona. If we lived on land, he would need a yard and a garage where he could putter around—we'd need to have a house, not a condo. Neither of us wanted to live in the suburbs. How would we afford a house in Chicago? Especially along the lake, which was the one thing we both agreed was a necessity. Chicago life can be gray, congested, unrelenting, unless you can see the wide, limitless expanse of Lake Michigan every day.

Mark liked the idea of staying in Chicago, of living on a bigger boat. He had fantasies of raising kids on board and kept telling me this was possible, that other liveaboards did it. He passed me magazine articles with stories about homeschooling kids on board in the West Indies.

Being married and living together in Anchorage—that made sense to me. But being married and living together in Chicago? I couldn't wrap my mind around it. Did I only want to marry Mark if we were going to Alaska? Of course not. But I did not want to live on a boat.

Besides missing the conveniences of modern life—electricity, hot water, freezer space—there was a huge looming issue about which we could do nothing: weather. When you live in a boat—even in the third largest city in the country—any illusion of security and consistency and dependability is gone. On a boat, you are always at the whim of the weather.

Sometimes it was pleasant, like a Sunday morning when Mark and I sat on the flybridge with the rain softly hitting the canvas bimini over our heads, listening to Mozart. There was a patch of pink clarity off in the east, but more rain clouds coming from the west. We stayed out as long as we could before retreating inside for the rest of the day.

More often it was like the Saturday night when my writing group met aboard *Mazurka*. While Mark captained us around the lakefront, Marcia, Germania, Julia, Lila, and I read from our works-in-progress, the sky growing darker with each writer. Marcia was just finishing her ode to Phil Collins when the sky erupted in thunder and the rain started coming at us sideways. We huddled together laughing, screaming, defenseless. Just as suddenly, the storm dissipated, the sky cleared, and the city shot off fireworks over Navy Pier. Later, back at South Hotel Ten, Mark doled out dry clothing to his guests. "You wouldn't happen to have a skirt, would you?" Julia joked. Mark disappeared into the bow and emerged with a white skirt. He had taken a sewing class to learn how to make curtains for his boat. All his classmates were women, and the assignment was to make a skirt. Mark made one for a classmate who never returned. It was white with a zipper; it fit Julia perfectly.

Or like the July night at the apex of a heat wave, when a party of friends came out to *Mazurka* to swim and escape the sweltering heat of land in the slight offshore breeze. A thunderstorm swept in out of nowhere. After weeks of suffering the heat, our party of ten refused to go inside, and we stayed under the bimini, eating wet grilled eggplant, watching lightning strike the masts of surrounding sailboats, until we finally retreated to the salon where the party continued, waiting for the storm to subside and the tender boats to resume service. By ten o'clock, the temperature had dropped fifteen degrees, and the tender boat arrived to pick up our party, now lifelong friends after surviving the storm. I still had my heart set on swimming, and as they motored off, I dove into the lake. It was ice-cold.

Swinging around a can in Monroe Harbor, the wind would suddenly shift and though we had gone to bed on a calm, glass-like lake, we would wake at 3 A.M. to a storm of torrential proportions. Mark would always wake up at the slightest shift in weather and run out in his underwear to make sure we were secure. I could almost always sleep through the storm, under the captain's protection and vigilance, except for one night when the storm interfered with my dreams, and I was sure Jesus was out on the bow, calling me to come out to him. I was too afraid, I stayed inside; in the morning I felt great regret.

By August, we stopped discussing the future, which is kind of strange for a couple about to get married. Instead, we dealt with the present moment, right in front of us: water, sky, varnish. I spent weekends with Mark at South Hotel Ten. I got up early to write atop the flybridge, watching other weekenders come out on their sailboats and eat breakfast. We would wave. I wore a Thai sarong even though it was getting cooler, the morning air resembling fall more than summer. Mark would sand the back hatch, working away to finish the varnishing with the deadline of cold weather looming. He was up in the middle of the night with anxiety about his day job; I would tell him to go out and varnish. At night, we would watch fireworks in the backyard and lie in bed listening to the near-dry water tanks beneath us dripping like we were spelunkers inside caves. In the morning, we would cruise down to Burnham Harbor, near McCormick Place, and fill up with fresh water. We would anchor out in front of the city and swim in the glittering, sunlit lake. Sometimes we didn't come in to shore till Sunday night when it was time for me to go back to my apartment. We seemed to be living in an alternative world—the illusive Chicago neighborhood almost everyone can see, few can visit, and those who do never want to leave.

Mazurka was slowly altering my perception of everything. She taught me nothing is permanently in its place; everything can be knocked off, slide off, slip to the floor with an unexpected wave. Spending long periods out on the water, even anchored in the harbor, I moved out of the workweek production mind-set into the "being" mind-set. I noticed the natural rhythm of the water, of the wind, how they moved together and moved us. *Mazurka* made everything more vivid.

I still had a lot to learn about boat life. Mark did things intuitively—"I'm just playing," he said, then described how he installed a switch so he could turn on the anchor light and the outside lights separately. I didn't know why he would want to do this, but I admired the fact that he knew how. "How'd you learn to do that?" I asked. He didn't answer. He was busy with his next project. He understood the way things flowed together on a boat in a way I did not. Everything on board affected everything else. Nothing was independent.

I began to feel that there were three of us in this relationship—Mark, me, and *Mazurka*.

One evening when we were swinging around the can, Mark gave me a small box. I closed my eyes to open it, felt the edges of the diamond with my fingertips: a single solitaire, one carat, princess cut, in white gold. It was the most beautiful gift anyone had ever given me.

In late August, we attended the Precana "Discovery Weekend," an intensive Catholic marriage preparation with twenty other couples. At dinner, the topic came around to where we planned to live. One couple in their thirties had her moving into his condo. "He said he didn't mind me bringing all my stuff," she said with some trepidation. Another couple was in their mid-sixties, the first marriage for them both. They were excited about the new condo they'd just bought together. Mark told them he lived on a boat, that we might live on the boat together. The man in his mid-sixties studied Mark a moment, then advised him with much seriousness, one groom to another, "You better get to condo hunting—quick."

Mark didn't specifically tell me that he really wanted me to live aboard with him. But I knew this is what he wanted. And I also knew that he knew I knew this, and we both knew it was asking a lot. Because it was asking a lot, I knew he wanted to honor his responsibility as husband and take care of his wife, make sure that she was comfortable and had what she needed. But he also loved his boat. He loved it more than anything else. I did not want to take him away from the one thing he loved more than anything else. But I was afraid of giving away too much of myself in this first compromise of marriage. I was afraid to live on the boat.

By September—that mythical month suspended in time, a second chance at summer granted for August days squandered in heat—I had succumbed to the varnish and began to help Mark in the pleasant late-summer sunshine. I was learning that *Mazurka* was an easy boat to love. She asked little and gave a lot in return.

But she was also capricious and dramatic. One gorgeous Saturday we invited Mark's colleague, her husband, and her father-in-law to come out for a ride. We prepared to cruise down to Burnham Harbor to fill the water tanks before they arrived. But the engine wouldn't start. Mark threw open the floor hatch and revved the engine, now visible through the open salon floor. He kept giving it gas and finally it started—and promptly spewed water and oil throughout the whole cabin.

Just then, of course, our guests arrived on the tender. We sat on the flybridge with them, talking about where we might have gone if the engine was running, and what could be wrong with it, anyway? Mark was naturally distracted, afraid that he had damaged the engine. Our guests left since we weren't going anywhere and the captain had work to do. Mark took the tender to shore along with them to buy engine oil. Who could guess when he might return?

The sun began to sink behind the skyscrapers. Alone with the boat, I finished varnishing and cleaned up, rinsing the paintbrushes at the kitchen sink. I had just started to wash some dishes when the faucet ran dry, and the cabin reverberated with the sound of the pump running continuously. At the console near the bow I shut off the water pressure as Mark had instructed me in the past. I tried to call him from my cell phone; it had run out of juice. Even if I had packed the electrical cord, I didn't know how to start the generator. I was stranded and isolated at South Hotel Ten.

Feeling a tinge of stir-crazy cabin fever, I took my laptop (with plenty of battery) up to the bridge, where I settled down to write, to distract myself, watching the colors of clouds over the city. A floating café of sorts. From the flybridge I could see the planetarium and Field Museum to the south, Buckingham Fountain to the north, and in between people walking, running, cycling, sitting with their legs dangling over the edge, or wearing orange vests and helmets, standing in the painfully slow march of Segways, the slowest walkers trying to get around them. The clouds drooped, drizzling rain; some people huddled under trees, some kept going. I listened to the drops on the canvas bimini above me, the rhythm old and familiar, and scanned for the tender boat. The rain passed, the lights of the city came on. I watched the sunset in the reflection on the cumulus clouds above the stratus clouds, stretched like cotton high above the highest buildings in the world. The city darkened; my computer screen swarmed with little bugs, and the spiders came out to spin their elaborate webs in every corner and crevice. It was quiet, still. My mind simmered down to a calm, reflective surface. I made my decision.

Mark returned on the tender boat. I went down to the deck to help him haul up empty ten-gallon buckets and five gallons of new oil, and more gallons of Lucas engine treatment fluid.

That night, he pumped out the watery oil into the empty buckets and set them on the deck, added new oil to the engine, and started her up. The fresh oil captured the white cakey emulsion that had collected in the engine from the mixture of lake water and engine oil (think mayonnaise); Mark pumped out that batch of oil into more ten-gallon buckets and changed the oil a second time. Then we called the tender to help us haul four ten-gallon buckets of dirty, greasy, watery oil to shore. Nobody can say I didn't know what I was signing up for.

A week later, Mark and I sat on the aft deck together, teak gleaming in the reflection of the last fireworks of the season over Navy Pier. Alaska was far, far away. Closer in our minds was the memory of the same weekend the year prior, when I sat on the bow watching fireworks burst right over my head, and he sat above at the helm, watching me.

"If you had told me last year this is where I would be," Mark said, "and that we'd be getting married . . ."

A whole lifetime had passed in that year.

"Do you think I spent too much time working on the boat rather than taking trips this summer?" Mark asked.

"That's what you like to do," I answered. "Have you ever taken a lot of trips on the boat?"

"Two," he said, "when I brought her from Racine, and Scott's bachelor party."

"Next summer," I said. "Next summer we'll go cruising."

A few days later summer turned; fall descended, dark, cold, and storming out on the lake. We stayed at my apartment for a week, then went out to see *Mazurka* on a Tuesday night. He wanted to check the engine after the rain, and take pictures of the sides of the hull, worried that the fiberglass was damaged. A summer in Monroe Harbor had taken its toll on *Mazurka*. We boarded the tender in a lull between storms, when it was only misting, the water calm and flat as it hadn't been in days; low gray clouds poured over the city, crawling out to Navy Pier, where they ascended and seemed to fall off the ledge of the Ferris wheel, disappearing into the lake. The boats in the harbor all faced different directions, as if they didn't know which way to go home, waiting for their captains to lead them.

The pouring rain started again as we neared *Mazurka*. On board, Mark tried to start the engine, but it wouldn't budge. This time, it wasn't a problem with oil; this time, there was water in the engine. He pumped it out and began theorizing. Perhaps, in the storms of the last few days, water had come in through the exhaust pipe, flooding the engine. "This boat may never have been out in rough water before," he said, recalling that on Sunday, there were three-foot waves in the harbor. He decided to lift up the exhaust pipe, to raise the mouth another foot. He took off his tie, rolled up his sleeves, and began sawing pipes.

Pretty soon he ran out of battery power. He stood scratching his head.

As little as I knew about boat maintenance, I had figured out that much of working on a boat is standing there, trying to figure out what to do. I also knew that this was what my soon-to-be husband liked best: problem solving. He never got short-tempered or angry, though he would smolder a low flame of anxiety until he figured out what was the real problem and what would actually solve it. Sometimes this took several attempts of several expensive possible solutions.

I was always a little uneasy watching him work on these problems—I didn't know enough to understand the problem, and I always wondered how he would figure out the solution, and what would happen if he didn't.

I asked him what would happen if he just left the exhaust unconnected to the engine.

"The cabin will fill with carbon monoxide and we will die."

He searched for more water flooding the engine, tried to start her again; a little smoke rose from the engine room. I feared the thing would burst into flames.

Often, secondary problems arose while the captain worked on the first problem. While he endeavored by flashlight to replace a burned-out relay to open the circuit for the starter that got knocked off, I read by dim battery-powered lamplight. I wished I had eaten dinner before I came out. I longed to be home, doing piles of laundry or the last-minute to-do items before the wedding in a week. Didn't I have vows to write?

Around eight o'clock, the rain stopped. We went atop the flybridge to take a break. The harbor was quiet, the lakefront barren, the city lights shining brightly now that the curtains of rain had been opened.

It occurred to me that one of the reasons I appreciated Chicago so much was because I didn't try to own it. There is a freedom in not possessing something—because there is no fear of losing it. I wanted to own Alaska, and I grasped at it, forcing it to fit into my cupped hands. I was desperate to not let it slip through, not drop it. We fail despite our attempts to hold tight, because we really own nothing—we can only admire, in whatever unknown temporary time we have in any given place, on any given vessel.

I wanted Alaska because I wanted adventure—and now I would be getting a different kind of adventure. I never would have made this venture had it not been for Mark. Living on a boat was not my lifelong dream. But I committed to living aboard *Mazurka* for a year. If I was miserable after a year, we would move to land. But I'd give it a shot.

My trepidation about moving onto *Mazurka* encompassed any

trepidation I had about marrying Mark. We would be newlyweds, learning how to live together like all newlyweds, how to give each other space yet still letting each other into our intimate lives—and we'd be learning it in a boat the size of a dentist's waiting room. A waiting room that rocked when the waves were high, that ran out of water and electricity, that had a disgruntled patient living in the basement who sometimes spewed oil everywhere and refused to start. Besides learning to share chores and manage a budget, we would have to learn to prioritize the mechanical disasters, how to move ahead, under stress, when resources were low. We would have to keep the boat afloat. This became my wedding vow to Mark: that I would stay with him through all the waves ahead, through smooth sailing and squalls, even when I'd rather be lounging on land.

On September 30, in a sea of impermanence, Mark and I made the one commitment we could: We pledged our lives together as husband and wife.

YOUR SALAD BLEW OFF THE DINGHY

On the second night of October—our second night as newly-weds—our sound sleep in Monroe Harbor was ripped open by a ferocious Canadian wind whipping across Lake Michigan, a nor'easter that bounced off the skyscrapers behind us and echoed back across the harbor, shoving us around the mooring can like a bully on a playground. *Mazurka* is tougher than she looks; she may get jostled, but she's not tipping over. Loops of lightning spun on the eastern horizon, spotlighting the cabin, followed by a great booming voice. I rolled in and out of sleep for hours, my stomach lolling with fear and uncertainty, my ears tuned to unknown items scurrying and sliding in the salon with each new push. I tried to imagine what each piece was as it slid across the floor, but I wouldn't get out of bed to check. The captain went instead, throwing on some warm clothes and a hooded jacket and making his way out to the bow pulpit, to make sure we were secured to the can but not ramming against it.

The next morning we woke to a calm lake, the surface a glassy, gray mirror, the surest sign that it had been a rough night and the lake was trying to make up for bad behavior. I went to the console near the bow to start the generator as Mark had taught me, turning off the battery power, pushing the button, waiting for the generator to rev. With electricity flowing, I ground fresh, dark roasted beans, plugged in the hot pot, and took my mug out to the deck to survey the damage.

Mazurka appeared unharmed. All around my new floating home, boats hugged their cans, facing every which way. The season was winding down—only two weeks left of harbor life—though more than half the sailboats remained. I looked out over the masts, searching for one that may have been struck the night before, leaving it crooked and bent, defeated, its boat sinking. But every one stood upright. The wind had shifted, coming from the south, warmer, scented with the final tassels of summer, the earth begrudgingly giving up the last of the harvest's treasures.

The next morning, we returned to real life. The wedding was over, our family had gone home; it was time to leave our private floating home for work on shore. Climbing out of the stateroom, I repeated my morning ritual and went to the salon to start the generator. Domestic rituals—especially in the morning—are important to me, and I delighted in my new role as first mate, proudly starting the onboard systems at the beginning of the day. I opened the control panel and turned off the battery power, then pushed the button to rev the generator.

It revved once, twice, three times. Stalled.

I pushed again: nothing.

The scent of coffee beans buoyed behind me. This was not good. I called the captain.

Mark appeared with a towel wrapped around his waist, revved the generator a few times, same results. Up came the hatch to the engine room—a sure sign this was trouble. With the towel still wrapped around him, he climbed down and disappeared beneath the floor. I hovered above, considering how to mash the beans with a pestle and heat water on the gas stove. "Can you hand me a flashlight?" Mark called from below. I grabbed one of four on the counter and handed it down. *You know this is how it goes,* I told myself. *This is not a surprise.*

I had learned in the year of dating Mark that, at times, things aboard just suddenly stopped working. Important things. Like the refrigerator, the satellite radio, the engine. To be honest, I didn't really comprehend just how many systems existed aboard *Mazurka,* how they all connected, or how much I would come to depend on them. When things beyond my comprehension inexplicably went dead, I had learned to step back and let the captain figure it out. He'd get it going eventually.

This was different. This was my morning cup of coffee we were talking about. This was serious.

Despite the four-foot waves, that evening, like many more to come, was spent with the groom in the engine room, patiently sweating over whether the generator problem was the fuel filter or the glow plugs or, worst-case scenario, the whole generator. Every so often he would pop his head out of the hatch beside his bride's feet. "Can you hand me the Phillips screwdriver?" I sat fidgeting, trying to read, eating sardines and cheese and crackers and olives, every so often reaching out to save a cup or fork about to slide off the table. I wanted to be helpful, despite the terrible inconvenience of the whole situation, and so I would hop up and search the drawers for the tool, wondering how I was ever going to fit into this life of a bachelor captain, with so many screwdrivers and lines and nets and fishing poles. The wedding gift from Mark's cousin Bob said it all: Our names and wedding date were inscribed on the handle of the Snap-on adjustable wrench.

While the romantic honeymoon would wait till December, our

real and immediate honeymoon was the journey of a captain intro-
ducing his new wife to his first love. Neither of us was sure how she
would react. Her first reaction: quit generating energy. Which is a
problem when you're still tied to a mooring can with no shore power.
Mark replaced the fuel filter; no go. He replaced the glow plugs.
Nada. He called his brother Ed, a mechanic in the UP, who told him
he could probably get it going with ether. Adapt, overcome, improvise. Ether worked.

Every time the cabin filled with the sugary scent of ether, I would
think of Hunter S. Thompson and his wise words on the way to Las
Vegas. "The only thing that really worried me was the ether. There is
nothing in the world more helpless and irresponsible and depraved
than a man in the depths of an ether binge."

Even with the chaos of a jealous first love, whitecaps in the harbor,
and a lack of electricity, my life had an exhilarating new focus. Mark
and I were married; we were undeniably together. The course may
be uncertain, but at least I knew the course was with him. The home
may be floating, but I had my home—with Mark.

He called me at work four days after we were married. "I just got
to *Mazurka*," he said through a cell phone line full of static. "It's really
windy. There are whitecaps in the harbor. I don't think we should
stay aboard tonight."

"Okay," I agreed, thankful we still had my rented apartment in
Bucktown. It would be no problem making coffee in the morning.

He added, "Your salad blew off the dinghy."

In a newly responsible attempt to forgo the restaurants of
courtship and eat at home like married folk, I had given Mark a head
of red leaf lettuce, broccoli sprouts, and sliced mushrooms to take
home for our dinner.

Standing in my campus office, watching the wind outside tangle newspaper and women's hemlines, I imagined our dinner flying off in a plastic bag over the lakeshore of downtown Chicago. Past the fading rose garden and Buckingham Fountain, past the overturned dinghies chained to shore and the orange-vested tourists on Segways. It escaped the jaws of the Sue the Brontosaurus outside the Field Museum, floated over the dolphins at the Shedd Aquarium, rounded the bend at the Adler Planetarium—a lettuce leaf whapped to the nose of Copernicus—and off—off to the factories and smokestacks of Gary, Indiana.

I hung up the phone wondering what I had gotten myself into.

The rotten weather meant we could stay in my apartment. But I knew it would clear up, and I would be faced with moving aboard. Not just a backpack, not just for the weekend. I had come to the precipice, the end of long, hot baths and chairs with ottomans. I'd been up front about my trepidation while trying to keep an adventurous zeal. But now my books and desk were bound for storage, and I had to decide which cooking spices I absolutely couldn't live without. Half my clothes were going to Goodwill, the other half into boxes until the seasons changed. Plants went to co-workers, furniture to anyone who would haul it away.

I was trying to remember the spiritual value of living a life of very few belongings. Because in a week's time, my life's satchel would be reduced to nine narrow drawers, a foot-wide closet, and a bathroom big enough to stand in.

OUR MORNING COMMUTE

On a cold, autumnal morning, the sky filled with brilliant sun, a line of cumulus clouds laced the eastern horizon of Lake Michigan. The southwest wind clanked while it turned generators atop fifty sailboats. We emerged on deck dressed for work—Mark in a tie and dress pants, me in a skirt and sweater—beneath waterproof jackets. At the stern, I held his briefcase and my backpack while he climbed down to the swim deck and pulled the dinghy from where it floated six feet behind *Mazurka*.

The dinghy was eight feet long, bought with Alaskan halibut. It sank at least once, in a storm; Mark came out in the morning to find it missing, then hauled it up on a line, and later rowed with one oar till he spotted the other oar floating a hundred yards toward the south end of the harbor. He never left the oars in the dinghy again.

The first time I climbed into the dinghy with its cracked sides and wobbly benches, Mark warned me, "If it sinks, it's going straight to the bottom."

He bought two inflatable life jackets to save us—thin, compressible, small enough for a briefcase, also able to inflate in that briefcase, which Mark learned when he accidentally pulled the cord at work.

The dinghy was a kind boat, a devoted boat, but untrustworthy, in the way you can't blame your clumsy friend for missing the free throw.

It was this boat—so small its name has been forgotten (though other dinghies earn such respect as *Bare Necessities* and *Half and Half*)—into which Mark placed his briefcase each morning before lowering himself in. I handed him the oars, he tossed me the rope, I gave over my backpack. Oars in place, bags secured in the bow, I climbed in and pushed off. I sat in the stern, facing my husband, legs together between his knees. We sat so close I could smell his tooth-paste and cologne. If it was raining, I held the umbrella.

The first leg of our commute was a half-mile straight shot through rows of tethered sailboats. Mark rowed, his back to shore, the Sears Tower ascending behind him, while I pointed him in the right di-rection if he got off course. If the wind was from the southwest, the water was relatively calm; from the northeast and we'd be waiting on *Mazurka* for the tender, late for work again. We glided past the *Ju-lianna*, *Sea Haven*, and *Top Gun*. The air was infused with color more than sound—the intensifying pink on the skyscrapers of glass, the lightening blue of water. No one would be out on the water so early on a weekday morning, but as we neared the shore, we were greeted by runners, and dog walkers, and the constant hum of traffic along Lake Shore Drive.

When Mark had a good clear path, I glanced back at our floating home, tethered to a mooring can in the middle of Monroe Harbor. *Mazurka* always appeared both humble and regal to me when viewed from the surface of the water. It was the most unexpected kind of home, with so much space and sky surrounding her. Limited and confined, this tiny floating home for us, on a limitless expanse of air and water.

We reached the cement wall. Mark steadied the dinghy while I climbed the ladder, unloaded the bags and the outdoor carpet (always

rolled in the stern of the dinghy), which I placed on the ledge to protect the boat as Mark climbed out and hauled it up. We locked the
oars inside, chained the dinghy to the metal loop beside its brethren,
flipped the tiny boat over.

We were downtown in a world-class city.

The first leg of our commute complete, we walked fifteen minutes
north along the lakefront to the Gold Wing parked illegally under
an overpass near Navy Pier, then hopped on for a fifteen-minute drive
to our West Side university offices.

People give all kinds of reasons for living on a boat: adventure, in-
dependence, a lifelong romantic dream.

For me, it came with a man.

SAFE HARBOR

In the second week of October, the wet cold of fall firmly entrenched, Mark and I went to see *King Lear* at the Goodman Theatre. At the beginning of the third act, Lear is going mad, raging against the elements, standing at the edge of the stage in an undershirt, rain pouring over him, howling, "Blow, winds, and crack your cheeks!"

You can't help but feel good for Lear in this moment, because he is free—free from his daughters Goneril and Regan, free from the political constraints of kingship and court life, free from the demands of who he is supposed to be. He is just himself—and whatever physical and spiritual strength is still in him—at the whim of nature. And even though it's a tragedy and we know he (and everyone else) is bound for the worst, I like to believe in that moment he just might win.

After everybody died and Edgar spoke the last word, we poured out onto the downtown sidewalk. It was bitterly cold and very late; the fountains broadcasting electronic faces in Millennium Park were dark, the taxis sparse; even the panhandlers had grown weary, not even asking for change. "She's beautiful," one panhandler told Mark as we passed him, "and she loves you." I hugged closer to my husband. By the time we walked the twenty minutes to the harbor, it was pouring rain; freezing drops hewn by the western wind stung our faces.

The harbor office was dark, the tender boats halted. We had to row home.

It's hard to explain why we would subject ourselves to conditions like this when there are perfectly good heated apartments available in every neighborhood of the city. Apartments easily accessible by stairs or elevators, some even with doormen to hold open the door and perch an umbrella over your head. Apartments with electricity just waiting to be switched on, bathtubs waiting to be filled with gallons of boiling-hot water, and steam radiators that hiss so much heat you have to open the windows, even in January.

But then again, these apartments don't have the thrill of riding the waves, of battling the elements just to reach the front door. There is no risk, no question of whether you'll make it. When we climbed down into the small rickety dinghy and pushed off into the storm, we left behind our daytime identities of career and citizen—suddenly we were lone humans in the world, trying to make it home. The goal was clear, the task arduous. This was the path of Thoreau, Nietzsche, London. Row on! The entire city huddled into warm high-rises behind us, and we surged ahead into the dark, freezing rain, the wind dragging and pushing us off course. Mark rowed, his back to *Mazurka*; I pointed and guided him to correct against the wind. Closer, closer, we were almost to the stern, *Mazurka* loomed above us, and I reached out with the hook to nab the swim platform. But the wind caught us, swooping us up and beyond *Mazurka*. Mark struggled to turn the dinghy, to row back to our home, but the wind lured our poor dinghy farther out. I suddenly didn't feel cold or wet anymore—I felt exhilarated! Would we be unable to row back? Would the wind take us all the way to the breakwall, where we would wait out the night in miserable wet solitude? Mark rowed harder, steering us back to home, as I tried to hook the stern of *Mazurka*, as it curved back and forth in the water, a whale not wanting to be caught. The freezing wind whipped snot from our faces, tears from our eyes, spewed icy lake water on us. I finally grabbed the tail of the swim deck, Mark grabbed the other end, and we scrambled aboard, tied the dinghy tight, and hauled the oars on deck. Climbing over the rail, we skirted the ice on deck and—without a working generator or electricity—spent the night under blankets in a cabin registering forty-one degrees.

I have always liked winter. And I knew it was coming. Like Lear, I knew I would lose. But as long as I had strength to withstand the cold, I would rage against it. "Blow, winds, and crack your cheeks!" I'd howl—'cause Lear didn't lose his sanity in the elements—he found it.

The harbor season was ending, and I didn't think much about where we were heading next. I figured Mark would know. One afternoon I met my husband coming out of the harbor office. "We got late-leaver status," he announced, waving papers in his hands. This sounded very exciting indeed, like something rare and special.

"Late-leaver status" is really just a way for captains in denial to pay a little bit more to stay a little bit longer in the harbors. For live-aboards who don't have to worry about putting their boats into storage, it's a great way to enjoy the end of the season at the lakefront. That year, we could stay an extra month in one of three harbors with water, pumpout, and fuel—Burnham, Belmont, or Diversey. As newlyweds, Mark and I were perpetually late. We also loved the idea of spending autumn in a new harbor. So as the geese flew south, we migrated north from Monroe Harbor to Belmont.

Belmont Harbor borders Lakeview, the North Side neighborhood home to Wrigley Field, Boys' Town, stores like "The Alley," very good theater productions, and a sprawl of restaurants so dense you can live there a year and never try all of them. The lakefront is packed with runners and cyclists and dog walkers. When I was a depressed, moody undergraduate at Northwestern in the mid-1990s, I would take the el from Evanston to Belmont Avenue, just to walk in Chicago and feel like I was a part of something kinda grungy, kinda hip, kinda cool. And now we'd be living in the park for a month of the most beautiful autumn colors.

We cruised out late Saturday afternoon, on the last day of the season, as the sun set behind the skyscrapers, the eastern sky a painter's palette of pastel pinks and blues. Just outside Monroe Harbor, Mark gave me the helm. I drove around Navy Pier, past the calm playpen waters east of the Hancock building, and out past the breakwall, heading north. The radio blasted the Animals' "We Gotta Get Outta This Place." The wind picked up, the waves rose higher, and I drove into them, aiming *Mazurka* farther to the northeast, my eye on the red light north of us.

We arrived in complete darkness and cruised our way inside the harbor, protected on the east by a peninsula of trees. The rows of docks welcomed us with their warm yellow lampposts. Most of the boats were already gone for the season, and we coasted right into the slip of our choosing on G Dock. After adjusting the fenders, tying up, and coiling the lines on the dock, we plugged into the relief of shore power. Then we walked right off the dock to the car we had parked earlier and drove downtown to see a concert.

Mark's modes of land transportation were just as unusual as his seaworthy one. In the summer, he drove his 1982 Honda Gold Wing motorcycle. But in the winter, he switched to his 1981 Delta 88

Oldsmobile, Brougham Royale, with bench seats, sagging slate ceiling fabric upheld by pushpins, and a trunk that really would qualify him for mafia affiliation. He bought the car from the mother of a colleague, who'd kept it in the garage for most of its life. Under Mark's ownership, thick white duct tape tacked up the passenger window and green Mardi Gras beads hung from the rearview mirror. It had been broken into twice; the second time, in the South Loop, the thief pushed down the passenger window and climbed in, broke the steering column, jumped it, drove it a block, parked it legally, left all his tools, and hightailed it out of there. Was it the rosary hanging in the dash? It was the kind of car immensely popular with a certain urban crowd; the kind of car that, when stopped at a light beside a car filled with six young men, the passenger would roll down his window and call to Mark, "How much?" The kind of car that his students, when he drove them to clinic sites, would joke about putting up fuzzy dice and fancy rims and pimping his ride. It is a mother of a car to drive in a Chicago snowstorm, a mother of a car you feel proud to parallel-park, a mother of a car that no one dare swerve in front of you when changing lanes on the expressway. Faced with the decision about which of our cars to keep in the marriage, I opted to sell my little manual Saturn and assume captaining the "Landboat."

That first night in Belmont Harbor, we returned from the concert near midnight to find a security guard parked at the entrance to the harbor. He flashed his lights at us. "My boat" was all Mark had to say, and we were waved in.

We slept soundly that night on calm water, protected from the waves and wind, and woke to sunlight and autumn trees. We ran along the lakeshore, later crossed LSD and the beautiful old high-rises to find groceries, then grilled tuna steaks with a view of downtown, the top lights of the Hancock darkened to make sure the geese found the right way to Florida.

The next night, returning from a movie after 11 p.m., we turned off LSD at Recreation Drive, turned right, and a found a big yellow gate blocking our entrance to the harbor. A sign announced park hours 6 A.M.–11 P.M. Mark hopped out in the pouring rain and checked the lock. Big yellow gate, big red sign, big thick lock. He got back in the car. I figured he'd turn back to the parking lot beside the tennis courts, and we would hoof it the half mile in the rain to the boat. He started the car forward—and then, in true yooper style, drove the Landboat up onto the curb and around the gate. Adapt, overcome, improvise.

Once we had the stability of a dock, it was time to move our last two crew members aboard.

Hunter and Leo—two brothers with long white hair, amber

spots, and ringed tails—had come home with me from the anti-cruelty society eleven years prior, when they were only six weeks old. They had traveled with me from apartment to apartment in Chicago; they had all of their claws, about half of their teeth, and had never been outside.

It's hard to tell which one was the alpha cat. Leo was more agile, more adventurous, more likely to pick on his brother. Hunter liked to lounge around on his back for belly rubs, and didn't always cover his business in the litter box. They shared their food.

Cats have lived aboard boats for centuries; they guard against rats. But I was skeptical these city cats would actually survive *Mazurka*.

We brought them at night and let them out of the carrier on deck. They roamed for just a bit before making their way inside. Hunter plopped in the middle of the bed. "So this is where you've been spending all your time," he seemed to say, and started purring. Leo retreated to a cupboard.

The following afternoon, in a brief window of sunlight, we brought them up to the flybridge. Leo crouched low, mewing, uncertain of the rocking or his footing, and returned to the cupboard. But Hunter stood tall on the flybridge, surveying the harbor, the wind blowing his fur. He looked like a true sailor cat, worthy of the high seas.

You never know how living on the water will change somebody—even a loafing eleven-year-old cat.

But sympathy pains got to him, and pretty soon Hunter hid in the cupboard with his brother. Every unfamiliar sound frightened them. When I came home from work, they stayed hidden away, rather than greeting me at the door. They hovered low to the ground, ate though they weren't pestering me for food as usual, and ceased

scrapping in the middle of the night. I worried they would never get used to boat life, even in a placid harbor.

Then one evening we started the engine and took the boat for a ride. I was certain this would send them over the feline psychological edge. They stayed in their cupboard the whole trip. Except at the end, Leo emerged slowly, with a familiar glint in his eye. We took him up to the flybridge, by the wheel, and he started to purr. He was just waiting to be captain.

Within a couple of weeks, they returned to their troublemaking selves, climbing up on shelves, browsing on deck, and burrowing in cupboards and the engine room as if they'd lived aboard *Mazurka* their entire lives.

My friend Denise—fellow writer, boater, runner, and cat owner—visited me on *Mazurka*. I introduced her to Hunter and Leo. "Oh!"

she said. "They're that one breed that loves water!"

They were both rescues, so who knew what kind of mutts they were. But later that day Denise emailed me with the name—Turkish Vans—and suggested I look them up online. I found pages with cats who looked exactly like mine: long white fur, amber spots, amber ears, and ringed tails. Hunter and Leo were indeed Turkish Vans.

Turkish Vans are known for loving water. The myth says they came to Mount Ararat aboard Noah's Ark and swam to shore. In modern times, allegedly, they swim for fun. Apparently Hunter and Leo had been waiting eleven years on land for the moment they could move to *Mazurka*.

With cats aboard, I had no more excuses to stay at my apartment. The peeling walls of four rooms closed in on me as I started the laborious process of reducing fourteen years of adult life to the very basics. I had moved there the year prior, from a three-bedroom into

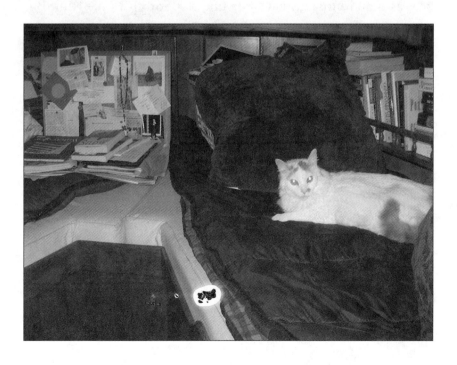

a one-bedroom, from a married life to a divorcée, and had given away a lot of things then. And I wasn't much of a pack rat. Still, I was a writer. I had a lot of what every writer collects: shelves and shelves of heavy books, and cabinets full of paper. I threw out blue bag after blue bag of college term papers and old Valentines. My books and journals were bound for storage. I tried to give as much as I could to Goodwill, and what furniture was left we lugged out to the alley, only to return in ten minutes with another piece and find the last piece already taken.

It's amazing how much stuff we don't actually need. After the dust and cat hair cleared, I walked away from thirty-two years of life with a dozen Rubbermaid containers, neatly stacked beside Mark's motorcycle in a storage unit downtown by the bus station. I had less stuff than when I left for college. You know what? I never missed it.

I half expected a forty-three-year-old lifelong bachelor to keep his boat as-is and insist his new wife find a spot to park her stuff. But Mark—generous, kind soul that he is—moved all the fishing gear, buoys, and tools from the forward cabin and gave the room to me. This was valuable, albeit small, real estate in a thirty-eight-foot boat. It was a typical V-berth in the bow of a trawler, a couple of steps down from the salon, where two beds converged at the front point of the boat and extended out in a V. Beneath the beds were empty drawers for me to put clothing. On the port side was a small bathroom with a toilet and sink. The starboard side held a closet. Two people could stand between the beds, if they were friendly. There was plenty of room for my stuff. My clothes filled the drawers and closet. On one bed I piled books, papers, and my bulletin board. On the other bed I would sit and read or write. It sort-of worked. Usually I just took my laptop up to the salon or the flybridge. Why write in a

V-berth when you can be on deck with the sky?

Aboard *Mazurka*, tucked in as husband and wife at last, we hid away from the world in our newlywed cocoon. For all my trepidation and worry, I fell in love with living aboard at once. I enjoyed the challenge of grocery shopping for a tiny galley, of trying to keep everything orderly, of puttering around and straightening up. I liked the simplicity of limited space. Yes, we had to clean every day, but there wasn't a lot of ground to cover. I loved our floating cabin, warm and snug in the late fall, Lake Shore Drive to the west and a view of the downtown skyline off the stern. We were in the city, but we were also in the middle of nowhere, with the expanse of Lake Michigan just to the east, curtained by red, orange, and yellow trees. We would watch the deep-red sunrise in the morning in a park empty of people, full of birds, with gray waves crashing against the shore, shooting up like a descending fountain against the concrete quay. In that pristine month, I had never felt autumn so closely, never paid such attention to the daily changing of leaves and wind, the earth slowly giving up its color to winter.

We were supposed to leave our autumn home in Belmont Harbor on November 15, bound for River City. That night, we drove home from work with two of our friends, ready for the move. It was windy all day, but not until we hit Lake Shore Drive and saw the lakefront like a pail of water lugged by a three-year-old did we realize just how windy it was.

We tried to convince ourselves it wasn't that bad, as waves crashed against the shore and shot twenty feet into the air. In the safety of Belmont Harbor, *Mazurka* rocked back and forth. I worried that the City of Chicago would fine us for staying in the harbor past the leave date. We listened to the marine weather report forecasting fourteen-foot waves. We hemmed and hawed. None of the other straggling boats in the harbor seemed in a hurry to get outta Dodge.

Finally, Mark declared, "I'm claiming Safe Harbor."

Safe Harbor. Who knew there was such a thing? Maybe because large bodies of water are the last wild frontiers: Gale-force winds can come up in an instant; thunderstorms, lightning, pirates. As we sat around the table that night drinking wine and eating dinner, Mark told us about his uncle Jeff sailing Lake Michigan when a storm came up. He parked his boat at the Great Lakes Naval Station, claiming Safe Harbor, and even though civilian boats aren't allowed there, they had to let them in.

What a concept: If you are in trouble, they have to let you in.

We stayed put for four more days, till the weekend brought smooth sailing.

We were reticent to leave the trees of Lincoln Park, but we got to

trade them in for giants of glass and steel. Now, instead of the constant hum of Lake Shore Drive traffic, we had trains and barges. Instead of watching runners gleefully racing outside on the bike path,
we watched runners like rats on treadmills in River City Bally Total
Fitness. I could sit in my home office and listen to the tour boat
guides all day. "And to your left, you'll see River City, which looks
just like the corncob of Marina Towers. That's no coincidence—they
were built by the same architect . . ." Moving to River City for the
winter, it was the first time in nearly a decade of living in Chicago
neighborhoods that I knew all my neighbors, the River Rats. It felt
good to be home.

IS THE PUMPOUT FULL? AND OTHER COMMON QUESTIONS IN THE LIVEABOARD HOUSEHOLD

When I told people I had just moved onto a boat, there followed a litany of questions.

First, the surprised look: "Can you do that?" (Yes.)

Then, in no particular order:

"Can you cook?" (Yes—both of us—and pretty well, actually.)

"How do you get your mail?" (PO box.)

"How do you wash your clothes?" (Laundromat.)

"Do you have heat?" (Yes: an electric heater, a gas furnace fueled by kerosene or diesel, electric space heaters, and we wrap the top in plastic.)

"Where do you get your water?" (Two tanks beneath the stateroom berth hold 150 gallons of fresh City of Chicago water and require filling every ten days or so.)

"Do you have a bathroom?" (Two, in fact, which is a blessing for newlyweds.)

"Can you take a shower?" (Hmm-mmm, albeit a very short one.)

And my favorite:

"Do you have a car?" (As if one mode of transportation was all we needed. I always wondered, do they think we're rowing to work? This question was always followed by the surprised look when we answered yes, and a motorcycle, too. And bicycles, buses, our feet, and the el! Who knew Chicago was such an easy town to get around in?)

To be fair, these questions are good ones. Nothing is simple on a boat, and a simple yes–no answer is rarely enough to explain the intricacies of cooking, taking a shower, or filling dry water tanks when the engine's out and you're tethered to a mooring can in Monroe Harbor. So for those of you dreaming the liveaboard lifestyle, here are some of the details to maintain the "simplicity" of daily onboard living.

Can you cook?

The first thing I did in my new role as first mate aboard *Mazurka* was rearrange the kitchen. I gave away the humongous microwave that took eleven minutes to heat a can of soup. I cleared out the pantry shelf and threw away half-used packets of meat seasoning and instant coffee from Thailand. I reoriented my culinary thinking, away from an apartment kitchen with a full-sized refrigerator and plenty of counter space, to a galley with a dorm-sized refrigerator, a gas stove with three burners and a small oven, a tiny shelf for a pantry, and two feet of counter space.

There wasn't a lot of room, but there was more than you might think, if you got creative and followed some simple guidelines.

We practiced the European style of grocery shopping, two or three times a week, which meant fresher food, and less waste. Ideally, we cleaned the refrigerator weekly. This almost never happened. More likely, we waited until the four-inch-high freezer was caked with two inches of ice and we couldn't close the door anymore and everything in the tiny freezer started to thaw. You'd think with a small refrigerator it would be easier to rotate stock and find what you need. Not so. With such a small space, stuff easily got crammed to the back, where

it sat for months. Or condiments seized the shelves. Stone-ground, honey, Dijon, wasabi, good old yellow—how many kinds of mustard did we need? A lot, apparently, considering the grill off the stern cooked dinner most nights, even in January. What the grill couldn't do, the six-quart slow cooker handled nicely.

We followed the collegiate theme. Along with the dorm-sized refrigerator, every boat's galley can benefit from the other staple of the collegiate kitchen: the hot pot. Use it to boil water for tea and coffee (and get rid of the coffeemaker), and to prepare any number of foods.

As with every space aboard a boat, none of it was wasted. In the colder months, we used the cooler on the aft deck for extra storage. On winter Sunday afternoons, Mark and I cooked meals for the week and kept them stored outside under the shrink wrap. It was a lot harder in summer when, without storage, we were faced with only buying and preparing what we would eat within three days. So after a long day of work when it was ninety degrees and the restaurant budget was tapped, we grilled or ate raw.

As little space as we seemingly had, we had an exquisite menu aboard *Mazurka*. Necessity is the mother of creativity and invention.

With small space, we were hyperaware of how much we consumed and how much we disposed. Garbage went to the Dumpster. Gray water from the sinks and showers pumped directly into the river or lake. (We used natural, nontoxic, earth-friendly soaps and detergents.) I was always aware that everything I poured down the drain would be floating outside my door in minutes.

Can you take a shower?

To provide hot water for your shower, your dishwasher, your clothes washer, the average house these days has a hot-water tank that holds thirty, maybe even fifty gallons of hot water.

When I moved aboard *Mazurka*, the hot-water tank held six gallons. Six.

Go to your refrigerator and pull out that gallon of milk. Imagine six of them on your counter; this is what you get for a shower.

The hot-water tank was electric, but when we were under way, the engine coolant heated the water. So if we were dockside and plugged into electricity, or just returning from a trip, those precious six gallons would be piping hot.

If you are a man with little hair, you can take a quick shower and be done with it. But you can see how this would be a problem if you were, say, a woman with long, fine hair—very fine hair that requires two rounds of conditioner. You can see how this particular woman might be screaming three-quarters of the way into her shower, and then avoid showering on the boat altogether.

"I can just go to the gym," I told my new husband.

The captain, wanting to please his new wife, began searching for alternatives. Shopping online, he found a cylinder that holds twelve gallons, a cube that holds ten. The cube was a great price on clearance but wouldn't fit in the engine room without knocking a hole in the wall; the twelve-gallon one cost fourteen hundred dollars.

"I can just go to the gym," I said again.

Early on Monday morning, I was poolside for the exercise, but really I wanted the long, hot shower afterward. When I stepped under the nozzle in the locker room . . . it was cold. Ice-cold.

Water, water everywhere—and none of it hot.

I told myself I was being environmentally conscious by taking six-minute showers. And after six months, I cut off eight inches of hair. The captain mourned it, but said he understood, with a tinge of guilt that it was his idea to live on this boat, anyway.

Quite unexpectedly, living on a boat brought out my girlie side. One afternoon I was sitting in the office of a client when I looked down at my hands: rough, worn, with torn, dirt-encrusted fingernails. I decided then that even though I lived on a boat, I shouldn't look like I lived on a boat. I vowed to keep my fingernails clean, polished, and sculpted, and my hands soft. (A scientist friend thought my dry, scaly hands were the sign of a genetic disorder. "No," I assured her, "I just live on a boat.") I started wearing makeup again and hanging up my clothes in the tiny closet so they wouldn't wrinkle in a heap on the bed. (There is so little space on board, you have to put everything in its rightful place, anyway.)

How do you do your laundry?

It doesn't take long for shipshape to become slipshod.

One of the first things to go is the laundry. We stashed our laundry in bags under stairways, where it could collect for weeks. In his bachelor days, Mark used to take his laundry to the River City Cleaners. When I came on board, I thought seventy-five dollars for two weeks of laundry was insane. Give me a roll of quarters and a few hours and I'll do it for ten bucks.

On a deceptively free afternoon, when the laundry was crawling out from under the stairs, I tore off the quilt and comforters, stuffed them into a bag, and proclaimed the laundry would be done. A week passed. We slumbered in a sleeping bag, laundry spilling around us. Mark suggested taking it to the cleaners, but I refused, saying it cost too much.

Finally, there was nothing left to wear. Mark piled everything we had into two huge bags and found a laundry just across Lake Shore Drive. The owner was amazed we lived on a boat, and promised to have it done by Tuesday. He didn't speak great English, and some things were lost in translation . . . but he said not to worry, he would take care of everything.

The laundry was a day late. "I've never seen so much," the guy told Mark on the phone. "I'm still working on it."

"What does he have to work on?" I asked Mark. "Just throw it in the washer and dryer and fold it."

The next night when I arrived home, Mark was waiting for me. "Is the laundry here?" I asked.

"Yes," he said. "You've never seen such clean clothes."

"How much was it?"

"Well," he said, "we're not taking any vacations for a while."

I started guessing. "More than a hundred dollars? More than two hundred?"

The grand total—at a 20 percent discount!—$380.

What did we get for $380? An amount that made Mark's hand tremble while he wrote the check, and compelled me to call the launderer and complain this was dishonest work that we never asked for? What did we get?

Every single item in those two bags was dry-cleaned and ironed. Including oven mitts, ball caps, and T-shirts. The launderer worked tirelessly to get oil stains out of Mark's work clothes and sweat stains out of my running shirt. The sheets were ironed and packed neatly into plastic bags. My underwear was safety-pinned to hangers in perfect descending order. He even included eleven pages of notes detailing his week's work. "Tried three times—sorry" was pinned to a pot holder that still had grease stains on it.

Our one and only time at Lakefront Cleaners resulted in the cleanest, crispest clothes we ever had on board.

"Everybody always wants dry cleaning," the launderer told me on the phone, apologizing (but not offering any money back—after all, he had the check in hand). "Next time I will know what you want."

There wasn't a next time for Lakefront Cleaners. We went back to rolls of quarters and waiting for seventy-five-cent washers—and we got a lot more humble about asking to do our laundry whenever we visited family.

For several months after, Mark was obsessed with installing a washer and dryer on the boat. He would wake up at 4 a.m. and research them online, deciding the combo washer-and-dryer-in-one would work. He was always pulling out the tape measure, sizing up the forward cabin, theorizing how he could pull out the forward bathroom counter, cut into my closet, destroy the drawers beneath the bunk. We would have clean clothes aboard, and no place to hang them.

One night I was in the forward head when I heard Mark just outside with the tape measure. "I think I found a spot," he called to me. "In the engine room, where the litter box is. We'd have to find another place for the litter."

"Are you really going to do this?" I asked.

"What—you don't want it?"

I thought for a second. A washer/dryer combo is expensive, bulky, troublesome to install, and quite frankly I didn't think it would really wash or dry our clothes. There were a million Laundromats in this city. For a drive across Illinois or Michigan, we could do our laundry for free.

"No," I said, "it's not worth the hassle."

He brushed it off. "I just like thinking about where it would go," he answered.

I did not believe him. He had an intensity of thought and a singleness of purpose that was admirable, but could also result in a huge washer/dryer sitting in the middle of the salon, too big to fit anywhere on the boat, reducing our twelve feet of living space to ten.

~

There were other questions common within the liveaboard household, including:

"What's that smell?"

"Where's this water coming from?"

And my favorite, often asked by the captain on his way to the head first thing in the morning: "Do you think the pumpout's full?"

If these three happen simultaneously, you know you're in trouble.

What's that smell?

In such a small space, nothing escapes the nose. You can stand in the center of the boat and know exactly what's going on and what needs attention.

You can tell when the sheets need to be changed, and when they are fresh. When dinner is cooking and when the refrigerator needs to be cleaned. When the bilge is collecting gray water, when the sewage is close to overflowing, when the heads are backed up. There's the slightly bitter, burning plastic scent of kerosene when we used it to fuel the furnace for a short time, and the softer, warmer scent of diesel when we switched to the less expensive fuel.

As people take on the scent of their homes, I wondered if I had become a walking diesel engine.

Where's this water coming from?

Every captain is intimately familiar with this question. When visitors come aboard for a tour, captains will often tell them the story of a leak: where the water came from, how he figured it out, how he fixed it—or how he's trying to. Captains have all kinds of advice for fixing and figuring out mysterious leaks. A caulking gun is never far from reach. Mark would fire it up and scour the boat, caulking at will. For months we endured a terrible leak in the aft stateroom; every time it rained, water would silently seep down the wall, mildewing and destroying books and papers beside the bed. We left the shelf bare—heartbreaking in a place with so little room—until Mark discovered that the caulking near the front of the flybridge was rotten. He deduced that rainwater was coming into the top deck through the flybridge, seeping down the length of the boat, and draining into the cabin through the aft deck. This sounded like a pretty big leap in logic to me, but he caulked and sealed the flybridge one weekend, and the leak in the aft stateroom stopped.

An important lesson I have learned living aboard: If you throw enough possible solutions at a problem, one of them will eventually work.

Then there are other kinds of leaks—preventable ones.

Is the pumpout full?

"Do you think the pumpout's full yet?" was a far-too-common question around our home, and oftentimes first thing in the morning.

Pumpout was our nickname for "sewage." *Mazurka*'s sewage tank held fifty gallons, and emptying it was the bane of our chores together.

Pumpout can be done alone, but it's really a two-person job, and one you can only do with someone you truly respect.

First, you must find a pumpout station, which any reputable marina offers. You will know it by the big white box, the yellow-and-black striped hose. Some marinas will charge you to pump out; others offer it as courtesy.

After tying up to the dock, attach the end of the hose into the sewage outlet port in your boat; on *Mazurka*, it was on the port side near the bow. (Do not mistake it for the fuel intake port.) Make sure you attach the hose into the sewage port before hitting the green button on the white box. This starts the suction, and you will feel the sewage pumping out. Some hoses even have a clear window so you can see it coming out. Wait until the tank is empty. Add some fresh water to the tank to rinse it; pump out again. If you are feeling considerate of your fellow boaters, coil the hoses neatly on the dock. Drive away with a clean tank.

In summer months, pumpout was not too difficult. After the engine warmed up, we cruised on over to the dock, tied up, put the nozzle of the pumpout hose into the spigot in the deck, and seven to ten minutes later the shit was gone and we were on our way.

Oh, were it that simple. Problem was, we never knew when it was

full, we were always guessing, and often we guessed wrong. We looked for telltale signs that it was full, like a gurgling noise, or a slower flush, or the fact that neither of us could remember the last time we'd pumped out. But the fact was that sometimes we didn't know it was full till it overflowed into the forward bilge, the small hatch beneath the floor of the bow, where two beds in the V-berth served as my office. The office started to smell like shit, and then the whole boat, and then not only did we have to pump out the holding tank, but Mark would have to haul the hose into the bow to suck out the overflow.

Rinse, repeat.

So Mark bought a sensor. He and his friend Carl hooked it up. It worked by two electrical wires suspended in the sewage tank which transmitted a current to identify when the tank was filled one-quarter, one-half, three-quarters, and then a red light flashed when we'd better empty it. But before it could work, it had to be calibrated to empty and full, and before we could calibrate it, we had to figure out when it was full. So every morning I checked the bilge for overflow, and we looked for the telltale signs. Except this time, there were no signs—two inches of sewage suddenly appeared in the bilge, and at 7 a.m. we were at the pumpout dock, Mark in the bow with the hose and some bleach.

I thanked him for doing the crappiest job possible while I waited on the dock. "This is the last time," I assured him.

I was sure there was a metaphor in all this, some metaphor about the first year of marriage. We were learning to handle our shit together, learning how to get rid of it and not let it overflow and stink up our life. I wished there was a sensor to let us know when the stress and anxiety of daily living was getting to be too much and we needed to pump it out lest it clog up our happy floating home.

Perhaps the first year of marriage is all about learning to calibrate.

When I told people I would be moving aboard Mark's boat just after our September 30 wedding, initial reactions ranged from "That's so romantic," to "Can you do that in Chicago?" Then they would ask, "What about winter?"

"We live on the boat," I would tell them.

"No, seriously," they'd say.

I would explain like I knew what I was talking about: "There's a heater, and Mark rigged up a furnace. It's insulated, and he wraps the whole top in plastic. There's a bubbler to keep the water circulating

around the boat."

They would look at me like I was crazy. "This is Chicago," they would remind me.

I would shrug. "Mark's done it for two years."

I started dating Mark during his second winter on board and even spent some January nights on *Mazurka*. It seemed like he had worked out most of the bugs of a winter aboard, so I felt confident that the freezing Chicago temperatures would not be our biggest challenge in our newlywed year.

But let's be honest: Before you spend a winter living aboard, you have no idea what you're signing up for.

The last week of November was sixty degrees. Mark and I rode a motorcycle back from the Upper Peninsula of Michigan, it was so warm. And then, it got cold. The wind blew. It got even colder.

How cold? My toothpaste was so stiff I couldn't squeeze it out. Cabin temperature fell to fifty-two degrees. The electric heater hummed nonstop; the gas-fueled furnace wasn't working. The captain spent hours toiling over it. The last pump to be sent was defective. When the next one came in the mail maybe Mark would be able to fix the furnace, maybe not. In the meantime, he sealed plastic over the inside of windows to stop the draft. Cabin temperature rose to fifty-five degrees. But maybe it was all the body heat inside.

The cats slept under the covers with us. We kept space heaters beside the bed.

Cabin temperature hovered between fifty-two and sixty degrees, when the sun was shining. Outside, it was twelve degrees, windchill one below.

My friends were concerned—everyone in the city was cold.

"How's life on the boat?" they would ask, preparing to offer their homes as refuge.

My friend and running partner Dorie, who had just bought a place in a Gold Coast gated community where the mayor's brother reportedly lived, had four floors and lots of windows and when I told her the cabin temperature was fifty-eight, she replied, "That's what we're keeping our place. Who would have thought they put single-plated glass in that house? Single-plated glass! It would cost a fortune to heat it. I don't even want to take a shower it's so cold."

Winter in Chicago is the great equalizer. Doesn't matter if you've got a posh place in the Gold Coast, or a boat on the river: If you're cold, you're cold, you're cold. The most any of us can hope for is a warm place to sleep for the night.

When Mark bought *Mazurka*, it came equipped with a Mermaid Reverse Air Heater/Air Conditioner, which his liveaboard neighbors told him would work as long as the water temperature stayed above forty degrees Fahrenheit. Below that, the electric heater would be unable to extract enough warmth from the water to heat the boat. (The Mermaid worked similarly to a refrigerator, extracting hot or cool air from the water and blowing it into the boat.)

Mark knew he wanted a backup heat source, as winters in Chicago can drop to subzero temperatures. Online research showed him his options to fuel a second heater were propane, electric, diesel, and kerosene. He wanted to avoid electric, since the Mermaid ran on electricity, and he wanted another system that would not rely on the generator if he were under way. He decided against propane because of the fire risk. This led him to buy a furnace that would run on diesel and/or kerosene; he decided on a Toyoset NS-2800 cabin heater, which he bought from Rural Energy in Anchorage. "I thought if a heater is sold up in Alaska, it's got to work."

Since the boat was already ducted, Mark decided to integrate the new heating system into the existing ductwork. The trick was to redirect the airflow from the Mermaid so it did not inhibit the hot air from the newly installed Toyoset (the Mermaid fan was twice as big as the Toyoset's).

He called a heating specialist in Chicago and told him he was trying to heat a room in his house—not a boat—with a separate heater. "I didn't want to tell him it was on a boat because every time I told a mechanic that I lived on a boat, they told me I had to talk to a harbormaster or a marine mechanic."

Mark told him he wanted to install a heater into the existing ductwork and just needed to know how to do it.

"The guy said, 'Why should I tell you? I do this for a living.' Then I broke down and told him, 'I'm really living on a boat and I'm all alone here on this marina. I'm a pharmacist and I have no idea what to do.' I told him I would pay him to do the work. He said, 'No, I don't do boats.' But he did tell me one thing: Air will only flow in one direction—the path of least resistance."

With that information, Mark was able to redirect the flow from the Mermaid by putting an insert inside the existing T-connection, which directed the airflow away from both heaters into the existing ducts.

Alone, the Mermaid could bring the cabin temperature to sixty degrees, which was colder than Mark liked. The addition of the Toyoset could raise it above seventy. Alone, the Mermaid would run continuously; with the Toyoset as a backup, the Mermaid could cycle on and off. For the first winter, both systems worked well together.

The Toyoset ran on both kerosene and diesel, though nothing specified #1 or #2 (which turned out to be a major problem later on). But for the first year, Mark decided to fuel it with the same fuel he used for the engine; he ran a fuel line through a Racor 120 filter and connected it to a diaphragm fuel pump, which pressurized the fuel to the heater, using the #2 diesel in the tanks. It worked. Over the first winter, the Toyoset ran continuously, burning about 150 gallons of fuel.

But during the second winter—with his new girlfriend hanging around—the Toyoset would not ignite. Dale at Rural Energy in Anchorage thought maybe it was the igniter, so Mark replaced it and the furnace worked for a while, then it stopped igniting again. More calls to Anchorage, and the Rural folks asked about the fuel. They had had problems with #2 diesel, which was what Mark was using. He sent the furnace back to Rural Energy; the fuel injector nozzle had carboned up, blocking the fuel from releasing into the heat pot. Rural cleaned it and sent it back, and it worked until spring, then stopped again. But by that point Mark had other challenges, like figuring out how to live on a mooring can in Monroe Harbor for the summer. Problems with the furnace would have to wait.

By the third winter, Mark had his new wife aboard with him. The winter was balmy for a long time, then dropped to a subzero windchill. Fifty-two degrees inside was chilly, but manageable. I kept reminding myself about people sleeping under cardboard beneath the Webster Street overpass.

The Mermaid hummed nonstop; the Toyoset would not ignite. Mark determined that it was not getting fuel. By now he knew how to clean the injector nozzle, which he did; no fuel. He replaced the Racor 120 filter, and the external fuel pump, which pressurizes the fuel line. No fuel. He diagnosed that it must be the internal fuel pump and ordered a new one from Rural; still no fuel. Mark methodically took apart the furnace a dozen times and still could not solve the problem.

We were saved in mid-December when a heat wave came through and the outdoor temperature rose to fifty-five degrees. We went on an Italian honeymoon over Christmas and when we returned just after New Year's, Chicago was sixty degrees. But there was the constant threat of another cold front coming through at any moment.

Ten days later, we left for the second leg of our honeymoon—a weeklong medical mission in Haiti.

Meanwhile, the guys at Rural deduced the motherboard was broken. They took pity on Mark and sold him a slightly used Toyoset at cost.

The furnace arrived, Mark hooked it up, and the sweet scent of Toyoset heat filled the cabin. (In my opinion, the heat from the Toyoset was much warmer and lasted longer.)

One important lesson was that #2 diesel would not work over the long term. The best options were #1 diesel or kerosene. Mark decided to give up on his elaborate fuel system and buy a two-and-a-half-gallon fuel tank, which he mounted in the engine room below the heater and filled with kerosene. The problem was that the kerosene was expensive and burned very quickly; a seven-dollar gallon was gone in twenty-four hours. So he got a twelve-gallon tank and went to the gas station down the street and filled it with #1 diesel at three dollars a gallon. One gallon of #1 diesel could fuel the Toyoset up to sixty hours.

It took three winters, but by February we learned that the balance of a Mermaid heater running on electricity and a Toyoset furnace running on #1 diesel was the key to a happy, warm cabin.

The mid-December heat wave was probably why, on the Saturday before we left for our Italian honeymoon, we still hadn't shrink-wrapped the boat.

Shrink-wrapping the boat in plastic protected it from the elements of winter. The plastic formed slanted walls that shed snow and ice; it prevented snow from accumulating (every foot of snow equals three pounds of pressure per square foot), and eliminated standing water that could freeze or seep into cracks and expand and cause damage. For a liveaboard, the shrink wrap provided a barrier to the wind, especially important in Chicago, and could raise the cabin temperature a good ten degrees.

For Mark, shrink-wrapping the boat himself was the only way to go. Paying someone to wrap your boat for the winter costs hundreds of dollars; doing it yourself makes up for the cost of buying the necessary gear.

"Dr. Shrink" sold a kit with an instructional video, a torch, a twenty-foot hose, a regulator valve for the propane can, and gloves. The torch had a trigger valve that created a very broad flame. The torch attached to the hose, which attached to the regulator on the propane can. Mark also needed a twenty-pound propane tank, safety glasses, a knife, and the material to wrap the boat: nylon strapping half an inch to one inch wide (a roll up to two hundred feet) and the plastic. The nylon strapping created the structural support for the shrink wrap and held down the edges of the plastic. Oftentimes strapping was used to create structures to hold the top of the shrink wrap, too. The plastic was best used in one sheet over the entire coverage area (all winter we watched as other boats, whose plastic had been taped together, suffered tearing and flapping, battered about by the wind). For *Mazurka*, a boat thirty-eight feet long by thirteen feet wide, we used a sheet of plastic eighteen by two hundred feet, seven mil thick (this roll lasted us two winters). Shrink wrap tape is powerful and very useful for securing the plastic to the boat (as well as holding up passenger-side windows after the Landboat was broken into).

The first and most time-consuming part of shrink-wrapping was building the structure over which the plastic would be shrunk; every boat had a different structure, depending on the boat and the owner's preference. The actual wrapping and shrinking of the plastic was relatively quick, once a good support structure was built. It could take all day to build the structure, a morning to secure the plastic around the boat, and an hour to shrink the plastic.

It's like setting the stage and rehearsing for a play; once you have the stage set, the performance is unfurling the plastic. The most critical point is unrolling the plastic over the boat and securing it down before the wind blows it away (Dr. Shrink recommends you never shrink-wrap in winds over ten miles per hour). With the plastic in place, tuck it under the strapping (which is wrapped under or around the perimeter of the boat) so that the edges are secure. It's like shrinking a shirt—the bottom has to be secured so that when it shrinks, it just tightens around your body, without rising up and exposing your navel.

The final step was to apply the heat with the torch, starting at the bottom and moving up, in a constant waving motion, like a marshmallow over a campfire. Make sure not to hold the torch in any place for too long (it will burn and melt the plastic). The colored or white shrink wrap can be helpful in this case (rather than clear), because you can see the ripples vanish and then you know the plastic is shrinking.

For liveaboards at River City Marina, shrink wrapping was an annual winter feat, where everyone tried to outdo last year's design and the work of their neighbors.

The first year Mark lived aboard, he had the flybridge wrapped by Thanksgiving. He used a bonnet design, covering only the flybridge, supported by wooden sawhorses. It was a sturdy design, but left the aft stateroom uncovered and drafty. The second year (in the midst of falling in love), he let the chore go until mid-December,

when a foot of snow fell in one day, and he panicked and pulled an all-nighter, wrapping the boat. The second time around, he built a base on the flybridge with two-by-fours, then used PVC tubing to suspend the shrink wrap on the flybridge and off the stern. But he secured the PVC tubing to the two-by-fours with zip ties rather than bolts, and during a big wind, the zip tie straps broke through the shrink wrap. He spent all winter repairing the structure and struggling to keep it from caving into the wind; good thing it never snowed again.

The second winter Mark also insulated the back stateroom cupboards with a ductwork insulation (foam with a sticky back), not to prevent the heat from escaping but to protect his clothes—they would get wet from the sweating hull and freeze to the sides of the boat.

The third winter, Mark had a new improved plan to build the

structure and cover the entire boat, stern-to-bow, and keep the windows clear. Since *Mazurka* has vertical sides, he wanted to keep the windows open, rather than create a shrink-wrapped bubble.

Of course, plans were always slightly ambiguous in my husband's mind, and on the Saturday before we left for Italy, he had me outside, holding PVC tubing while he torched the middle to curve it, all part of an elaborate crown design for the flybridge. By midafternoon when our friend Dennis arrived to help, it was obvious there was no way PVC tubing was strong enough to suspend the heavy plastic, and we went with a simple yet effective revision: five tall sawhorses, hinged at the top, built on six-foot two-by-fours, three atop the flybridge, one at the bow, one at the stern. The design was perfect in its simplicity; River Rats came out to applaud.

But we spent so much time on the structure that we ran out of time to actually wrap the top in plastic. We flew to Rome for our

honeymoon, then spent another week in the Dolomites, where they were trucking in snow for skiers. The talk everywhere was of climate change. We returned home on New Year's Day to sixty degrees.

To wrap or not to wrap? Many River Rats weren't going through the hassle. Mark asked my opinion; I told him I thought it was a waste of time. "Of course, it could drop below zero next week," I said. "This is Chicago."

So the next Saturday, a spring-like day in early January, Mark was out testing the blowtorch before I was even out of bed. Soon I heard him calling from the dock, "Can you come out here a second? I just need you to . . ."

Ten minutes later, I was dressed and standing on the flybridge. Mark was perched on the dock in front of the boat, a four-foot roll of plastic balanced across two deck chairs before him. Slowly, he unrolled the plastic, sending it up to me and down the flybridge until the entire boat was draped in a thick white blanket. I stood beneath the plastic, the air around me still, the downtown sounds muffled; I felt like Jonah, peaceful and safe in the belly of the whale. *This isn't so bad*, I thought, arms high above me to hold the plastic, *I like helping my husband . . .*

And then, as it often does in Chicago, the wind changed course and a frigid gust blew up the river, up under my secure blanket of plastic, and suddenly I was holding on for dear life to a parachute I could not control. It turned under like a tidal wave while I fought to keep the plastic from diving into the river water and taking me with it. Below on deck, Mark raced around, trying to secure the plastic under the white strapping around the bow and above the windows. But as soon as he tucked up one side, the other side blew out. Stan the Man appeared—"I couldn't watch you guys do this for much longer," he said—and he and Mark taped the plastic to the sides of the boat while I steadied the top. Once the plastic was securely tucked under the strapping, Mark tied the blowtorch to a gaff and in a few hours the marshmallow top was heated and sealed down tight—not a single bit singed. The entire bow, flybridge, and aft deck were covered, along with the aft cabin windows. Just behind the bow, Mark cut the shrink wrap and taped it along the sides leading up to the salon windows, where the strapping began and the plastic could be secured above the windows, leaving the salon windows and walkways open. We also covered the tops of the two-by-fours in lots of tape to prevent the sharp edges from piercing the plastic.

A week later, the temperature dropped to the single digits again, and I was sure glad my husband had the foresight to wrap the boat.

When we returned from the second honeymoon leg in Haiti, we spent January snug inside our cabin igloo, enjoying seventy-degree temperatures and a view to the outside. Mark cut a zip-door into the stairway to the aft deck so we could access the cooler (a convenience of winter is increased freezer space). When it snowed, I shoveled the narrow walkway with a dustpan, and climbed up on the flybridge to pat the snow off the plastic. The top stayed tight, even when the wind blew, while elsewhere in the marina plastic blew off boats like abandoned kites.

By early February, we had managed a broken furnace, survived a heavy snowfall, and perfected the art of shrink-wrapping. It seemed smooth sailing till spring.

In early February we drove to the UP for the annual Ice Fest, a long weekend of cross-country skiing and climbing frozen waterfalls in subzero temperatures.

You have to really love the cold to want to climb ice. It requires putting on several layers of clothing, procuring the necessary gear (harness, crampons, ice axes, helmet), and hiking out to a frozen waterfall. Walls of ice are unforgiving, and don't much care how fit you are or how far you drive to climb them—they are cold and foreboding and will stand firm no matter how much ice you chip off in your attempt to scale the wall and conquer it.

We were exhilarated Sunday night, driving back to Chicago, counting down the temperatures ("Now it's eight below!"). We returned from a weekend climbing ice to find . . . ice. It was something neither of us had ever seen. The Chicago River was completely frozen over, with geese like new penguins sliding around on the interlocking triangles of dark black ice. The River City Marina was solid; ice closed in on *Mazurka*'s hull so that it resembled Shackleton's *Endurance* at the South Pole in 1915.

We opened up the door to find a frigid tomb. Inside, the cabin temperature was twenty-eight degrees—everything was frozen, including all the faucets, pipes, olive oil, shampoo, and contents of the refrigerator. It felt like an abandoned ghost ship, save for Hunter and Leo, their fur puffed up, looking a bit shell-shocked and thirsty—their water dish was a solid block.

I called my ex-husband (I had asked him to watch the cats over the weekend). When he came aboard Saturday afternoon, everything was fine. We deduced that sometime in the previous twenty-four hours, the Mermaid heater had stopped working, probably when the river temperature became so cold that the water inlet froze and the heater could no longer pull in warm water to heat the boat. The Toyoset furnace (which Mark had just begun fueling with kerosene, before solving the diesel issue) roared through the fuel in less than a day and also quit.

"This is my worst nightmare," Mark said. He started the engine— the quickest way he could think to warm things up. (We never winterized the boat because we always kept it warm; maybe a day more and the engine would have frozen.)

We heard the terrible crack of a pipe breaking; thankfully it was just the drinking water filter under the sink. Expensive, but not dire. We stayed up till 1 a.m., when the cabin temperature had risen to forty-two degrees, then went to bed on an ice-cold mattress over the water tanks, which were probably frozen, too.

While I love climbing frozen waterfalls as much as the next girl, I like it even more when I know at the end of the day, we're going to hike back to civilization and back to the hotel, where there's hot soup and coffee and a sauna and whirlpool. Driving eight hours back to Chicago, I was looking forward to a luxurious six-minute shower, some clean clothes, and a warm bed. Instead, we lay down on a block of ice wearing the same three layers of clothing and hats and coats we'd worn all weekend. I tried to be grateful that I had a roof over my head when there were plenty of people sleeping under cardboard. It was all I could do not to break down sobbing.

"I feel like throwing up," I told my husband in the darkness. He agreed. It was the first time in four months I thought maybe living on *Mazurka* wasn't such a great idea.

The next morning we fretted about living aboard without water. We considered which friends we could stay with. Mark said he would stay on *Mazurka* to make sure she was okay. I wanted to put my cats in the car and drive three hours to my parents' house till things heated up, but I thought again; I was married now—I would stick by my husband.

After his return to Britain, Shackleton related the sound of ice squeezing the *Endurance*, locking it in a vise that eventually forced the crew to abandon ship and haul lifeboats across the frozen Antarctic tundra. It was one of these lifeboats that Shackleton and a few crewmembers sailed on an amazing voyage to get help and save the entire crew.

I doubt any of that crew ever forgot what it was like to walk away from the *Endurance*, abandoning her to the ice.

"What's the worst that could happen?" I asked Mark.

"A pipe could burst and the boat would fill with water and sink."

So we sat with *Mazurka* all day. We kept the engine running and space heaters cranked and bought two more space heaters. By midmorning we were up to fifty degrees. Mark used an auger to cut a hole in the ice near the bow, then built a contraption off the dock to suspend the de-icer beneath the bow of the boat. The powerful fan began churning the water, fighting to keep the ice from squeezing the hull and potentially cracking it.

Ice damage to the hull can range from small permanent dents to fractures of the boat's side structure. In compression ice like we experienced, a boat stuck in the ice can suffer damage in the midship areas of the flat side region.

For fun, and because it looked possible, I decided to test the strength of the ice off the stern and stepped right from the swim deck onto the ice. It held. Cabin temperature kept rising. By late afternoon the pipes had thawed and we had water again, but drains stayed frozen. We decided it was safe to turn off the engine.

That night, we slept in a warm bed, listening to the reluctant moan of ice as it released its grip on our home.

By the next afternoon, cabin temperature was seventy-one degrees, and we had hot water and functional plumbing again. The powerful de-icer had cleared all the ice from the boat, and from every boat around us. Hunter and Leo basked in their new sources of heat. Outside it snowed, and the windchill remained below zero. By the next day, we were floating again.

When I told my friend Anne our adventures, she laughed. "Instead of trial by fire, you're going through trial by ice!"

The winter remained unseasonably cold through March, and in addition to the Mermaid and Toyoset, we kept the four space heaters cranked at all times—one in the engine room, two in the bedroom, one in the cold bow. (Maybe it was excessive, but we didn't want to take any chances of a repeat *Endurance* experience.) The shrink wrap didn't come off till the end of April, right around the time that cabin fever hit hard.

You'd think we'd had enough excitement for one winter. But a last nip of liveaboard adventure still awaited us.

Word on the marina was that the pumpout was broken. It had been a good two weeks since we pumped out, but when we heard the news from Stan on Sunday, we didn't take it too seriously. A fellow River Rat had tried to pump out to no avail. "Too bad, 'cause he's full, too," Stan said. We agreed. Too bad. We went on our way.

Monday, we noticed some overflow in our bilge. Probably from the condensation that formed ice inside the boat and was now melting. It wasn't very dark. But by evening, it was dark. And smelly. And Tuesday morning, the toilet was resisting when we tried to flush it. Yep—time to pump out.

If pumpout was a two-person job before, winter complicated it tenfold. Mark would walk through the back alley to the opposite side of the marina and stand on the opposite dock, separated from

Mazurka by the entrance to the marina, about twenty feet across. I stayed close to our home, and would toss Mark one end of a yellow rope (the line for a water-skier, actually), which he tied to the pumpout hose. With the rope, I would drag the hose across the marina to our side. It just reached the opening to our tank, and I would attach it tightly while Mark flipped the switch of the pumpout unit. We communicated by yelling across the marina; if it was windy, we used cell phones.

(One late-autumn night, trying to surprise Mark with a gift, I attempted this process all by myself, trekking back and forth through the dark back alley to get from one side of the marina to the other. I managed to fling the rope across, tie it to the hose, and haul it back over, but couldn't get the pumpout switched on. Our fellow River Rat Oz came out to help. Turns out the pumpout was broken that time, too.)

That cold winter night, after shoveling a foot of blowing snow off our deck, I tromped through the back alley to the pumpout, to find it covered in duct tape with a sign: OUT OF ORDER MANAGEMENT CALLED. When Mark came home, he thought he could get it to work; he couldn't. We had a full tank, a nonfunctioning pumpout, and a snowstorm so bad that they were canceling university classes.

Mark made some calls. The River Rats all said the same thing: "I'm peeing in a bucket." He called Captain P, who was vaguely in charge of marina management. Captain P said he outsourced the marina management to a great company—but they were on vacation for three weeks. The hose was probably frozen—just gotta wait till it thaws out. And the fact that temperatures were supposed to drop below zero for the next week? Captain P shrugged over the phone. "I'm peeing in a bucket."

Mark relayed all this to me after he hung up the phone.

I repeated it to make sure I understood. "You mean the guy in charge of the marina is peeing in a bucket 'cause he outsourced the job of fixing things and the company he outsourced it to is on vacation?"

Mark confirmed this to be true. "The entire marina is peeing in a bucket."

We did this before, you know. In the big freeze, we went without water and peed in a bucket, and came up with an ingenious design of a plastic bag in the toilet to catch our solid waste, which we promptly threw out in the same Dumpster beside the little bags of dog poop. (Mark claims he never did this. He went to the gym.) It's not like this was new or anything.

"I don't want to pee in a bucket," Mark said. "It's the principle of the thing."

I asked him if he could just leak the waste into the water. "I'd do it if we were out on the lake, but I don't want to do it in the marina."

We discussed the options. There weren't many. Mark got a scary look in his eye. "How about we just get a shop vac and suck it out? I won't throw it in the marina, but I'd throw it in the river."

"Maybe you should sleep on this idea," I suggested.

Our sewage tank held fifty gallons. "If we had a ten-gallon shop vac, it'd be five times flushing it out," Mark reasoned. "If we had a twenty-gallon shop vac, that'd be half of it. You don't like this idea, do you? C'mon, baby, where's your sense of humor?" But I knew he wasn't kidding. "Trying to be self-sufficient, too, you know?"

"You don't have a problem emptying fifty gallons of raw sewage into the river?" I asked.

"Hey, it was your idea," he said, "but I am a member of Friends of the River. I took an oath and all . . ."

So we peed in a bucket. And found toilets in restaurants, libraries, and office buildings as often as possible. Who knew when this problem would be solved? The trickiest part was nobody really knew who was managing the River City Marina. River City? The condo association? Captain P? Some mysterious outsourced company?

The best thing about living on a boat? You're under the radar. The worst thing about living on a boat? Still under the radar. Just remember to bring your bucket.

After almost a week of fruitless phone calls, Mark did what any good liveaboard does: He took matters into his own hands.

The marina's pumpout hose snaked down into a manhole that led to the sewer. Mark deduced that the hose was frozen about twelve feet down. So he connected a handful of extension cords and suspended a ceramic space heater down the manhole and melted the proverbial rat in the snake's belly.

Adapt, overcome, improvise.

The pumpout was working in less than an hour, and *Mazurka* again smelled like lilacs. Well, lilacs in a diesel gas station.

In the spring people congratulated me on surviving my first winter on board. "If you can do that, you can do anything." I endured a lot of compassionate smiles. "So many times when the storm was blowing, I imagined you guys out there on that boat . . ."

To be honest, it wasn't all that bad. Adversity brought us closer together—Mark and I learned a whole lot about each other during those frigid months. I wouldn't trade anything for close evenings in the cabin while the wind howled and blew snow all night.

When looking at a winter aboard, the biggest question to consider is how adaptable you are—if something breaks or goes unexpectedly wrong, can you put up with a little discomfort while you figure out how to fix it? But that's always the question for a boater, whether it's eighty degrees and perfect sailing or below zero and storming. And really, that's why we do it, right?

For a winter aboard, a tight, secure shrink wrap, an electric heater, diesel-fueled furnace, space heaters, a heavy quilt, two cats, and the one you love will keep you warm all season.

And when it snows, you can shovel the deck with a dustpan.

MY HUSBAND'S MISTRESS

Newlyweds study a new language—the "look" of their beloved. A "look" is not just the facial expression, but includes gestures, posture, and the subtle, almost imperceptible context that only a spouse can discern. Or would like to think they can discern.

The study of looks starts with the "Wow! We're in love! Who knew the world could be so wonderful?" look and the "I can't believe someone as amazing as you exists!" look. My introduction to this new language also included the "I'm so distracted by you that I notice nothing else, not even that I'm about to miss my flight" look. These

can be very enticing, and somewhat deceptive looks. Novice linguists have to be careful not to assume that this limited vocabulary covers even a tiny percentage of the language they are about to study.

After some time, the newly smitten may notice some other looks, looks that have absolutely nothing to do with them, such as the "I just had a rotten day at work and I need to sit on the throne with the newspaper" look. There's also the "It looks like I'm listening but I'm not taking in a word you're saying" look (note the close proximity but complete lack of response to sentences repeated at louder volume), the "Get out of the way I'm on a mission" look (arms pumping, legs striding, gaze intent), and the somewhat disappointing "I'm exhausted and going to bed early" look (snoring).

The newlywed liveaboard dialect includes the excited "Scratched varnish? New project!" look, and the focused "I don't know how to fix this thing but I'm going to keep trying till it kills me" look.

(Not to be sexist, but in my experience, husbands aren't into studying this language nearly as much as their wives. And I'm not saying all wives do this, either. So let's just say it's me. In our first year of marriage, I was always rummaging for what was going on inside Mark's head—a place I had no business being, mind you. Mark has told me that he only knows two of my looks: "I'm upset," and "I'm happy to see you.")

The newlywed makes a crucial error if she forgets this study must be done covertly. Her request for clarification, "What's that look mean?" will likely get the response, "I have no idea what you're talking about." Her attempt to reveal her new understanding, "You look like you're in a bad mood," will get the response, "I have no idea what you're talking about."

The novice linguist is best off filing her reports in secret and keeping her mouth shut.

My least favorite look of Mark's was the "Saturday morning" look. It was consistent, for sure, appearing early every Saturday morning, popping him out of bed, propelling him purposefully about the cabin. It meant a project or a field trip. Best-case scenario was an excursion somewhere fun. Worst-case scenario was varnishing or pulling apart the entire engine room to paint the floor or—the most dreaded—disappearing down the dock with his toolbox. An important facet of the "Saturday morning" look, which I learned quickly, is that it always needed an accomplice. This is great if a motorcycle ride is in store; this is torture if it means lying cramped between the engine and the generator holding a flashlight for an hour.

In the first spring of our marriage, I spent three weeks traveling. I was gone so much that every toiletry I owned was in a three-ounce container and I spent a week in every time zone in the Lower Forty-Eight. On only one of these trips did Mark and I go together. So our seventh month of marriage was a lot of phone calls and happy reunions.

While I was away, Mark reverted to "bachin' it." Bratwurst and scrambled eggs for dinner, staying late at the office, spending a lot of time fixing up *Mazurka*.

On my last trip away—Jill's baby shower in Detroit—I spent five days with Mark's family, without him. He and I talked morning and night, mostly about how he was getting the boat ready for me to come home. I could hear a new look over the phone: "Proud provider prepares homestead for wife." He took off the plastic shrink wrap, scrubbed and buffed and waxed the deck, repaired and hung the bimini, stowed all the space heaters and other winter gear in storage.

On Sunday morning he was drilling holes. "I'm working on the sink that doesn't drain," he explained.

"What sink?" I asked. To my knowledge, there were no problems (yet) with any of the sinks.

"You know, that one in the kitchen that doesn't drain—the thing that always stops the water."

"You mean the dish strainer?"

"Yeah—that—I'm drilling holes in the bottom."

I was flattered he missed me so much he was drilling holes in Rubbermaid.

When I returned Tuesday afternoon, *Mazurka* looked beautiful. Mark came home from work, and after the big kiss and hug held up two small bags before me. Inside, there was gold. "Here they are," he said with great satisfaction. He opened the bags, revealing two gold couplings—the pieces for which he had been waiting to fix the generator.

Perhaps if Mark were as interested in my looks as I was in his, he would have noted the blatant "Mild disappointment" on the face of his attention-seeking wife.

We went for a walk at the lakefront, came home, made dinner. A recurring topic of conversation swam between us—would we ever move back to land? Would we move to a condo, the suburbs, another city altogether? What would happen to *Mazurka*? After three weeks traveling, spending time with families and babies and houses, I had new frontiers on my mind. Could we raise a baby aboard? Not likely. You can't have a baby crawling around the salon, and where do you put a crib—on the flybridge? The poor kid would grow up permanently ensconced in a personal floatation device, his arms bowed and his chest puffed like a bodybuilder. Even if we didn't have kids, I was growing tired of the constant maintenance the liveaboard life demanded. The next breakdown was always a key-turn away, the next expense trenching deeper into our savings.

People sometimes told me, "Oh, living on a boat? You must be saving a lot of money." These people had no idea what they were talking about.

"One thing's for sure," Mark said, with love in his eyes, "she needs to be in the water. She can't survive if she's not in the water."

It took me a moment to realize that he was talking about the boat.

A new look for the first mate: "Resigned deference to the first love." Could also be interpreted as "Resentment."

Right after dinner, a more commonly occurring look appeared on Mark's face, one that I was beginning to recognize by the way it washed over me as if I weren't there: "Fixing *Mazurka*."

At ten o'clock, I bent down into the engine room to kiss the top of his head on my way to bed.

At eleven o'clock, I was woken by several unsuccessful attempts to rev the generator and the sweet scent of ether.

I went to the doorway of the salon. "Mark," I called down into the engine room, "I haven't been home in a week. Can't you come to bed now?"

"I almost got it . . ." he called.

I closed the door to the stateroom and went back to bed. But the little devils scurrying in my mind kept me awake with their busy seed planting. "He doesn't really love you, he loves the boat. He didn't miss you at all, he just wants to be alone with his boat." I didn't give in and I didn't pout and I didn't start an argument. When Mark finally came to bed, he put his arm around me and started to snore.

By now I was wide-awake, thinking.

My biggest fear moving aboard *Mazurka* was that I would be living on a project. And truly, that's what it was—Mark's epic. My husband loved his boat. I was gradually learning that despite his anxiety

and stress whenever something broke down, he loved the challenge of figuring out the problem and solving it. There was no shortage of problem solving to be had. As soon as the generator was churning electricity, the water pump began sounding strange. We triumphed over winter only to get the problems of summer.

I could relate to the way Mark loved the problems of *Mazurka*. He felt toward the boat the same way I felt about writing. I hated the challenge as much as I loved it, and as much as I complained and paced anxiously about a piece that wasn't coming together, I wouldn't trade it for anything. Mark respected my writing more than I did; I should at least show him the same reverence for his beloved projects.

There was a quote taped to my computer attributed to Joseph Conrad: "I don't like work—no man does—but I like what is in work—the chance to find yourself."

As I lay in bed beside my sleeping husband, I had to remind myself why I liked living on *Mazurka*. It was the most creatively stimulating thing I had ever done. Everything was in chaos—the unexpected could happen at any moment, nothing was ever guaranteed, and lest we ever think the floor beneath us was solid, there were daily reminders that it was only through the grace of God that the whole thing didn't sink.

I adored so many of the unexpected gifts of liveaboard life. Waking up and looking out over the water surrounding us. Falling asleep to the gentle rocking of the boat. And the best moment of all—when we would take up the lines and push off. Suddenly we felt a different pull: the pull of water, the pull of a story—we forgot we were ever tied to land; we forgot there was ever a time we weren't free.

In River City, with shore power, we didn't need to worry about a generator. And with all the challenges that winter sent our way, the generator issue took a back burner until the onset of spring, and the knowledge that on May 1, we'd be headed back out to Monroe Harbor.

The generator problem moved into first place. Mark got the name of a guy who worked on generators. He called him on Saturday; Paul came on Sunday. He was a surprisingly young kid, but pretty nice, and as he bent down in the engine room to examine the problem Mark gave him the detailed story of everything he'd done to try to fix the thing. Paul said he had to come back the next day. We were gone, but he came by, and later called Mark to say he had to take the lift pump to test it. He called again to say he tested it and it didn't work, and told Mark he had to get a new generator. Paul offered to look into it. He called a third time to quote him a price of a new generator, plus warranty, plus installation, all for a meager fifteen thousand dollars. Mark said he'd get back to him.

My husband checked online and found generators that were less expensive. He also posted the problem on a boaters' site; fellow boaters (the good community they are) responded in droves. "Sounds like you need a new mechanic," was the consensus.

Mark broke down and called Onan, the generator manufacturer. They charged four hundred dollars to send a repair guy for two hours. But compared with fifteen grand, it didn't sound so bad.

Dave from Onan was over six feet tall, a Harley guy, with tattoos up and down his arms. The first thing he said when he walked in the door was, "Do you have an attack goose out there?"

Dave found that it was the injector pump—which the Midwestern Injector people rebuilt for less than four hundred dollars, finding a broken spring that prevented the pump from opening and closing.

When the rebuilt pump arrived, I was out of town. Mark was excited to put it back together and get it running before I returned. He was hunched down in the engine room, reassembling everything the way Dave instructed him, with his brother Ed on the line for consulting.

"I had all these washers and these injectors," he explained to me when I returned, "brass washers, aluminum washers, there was a washer with holes in it—I couldn't figure out why a washer would have holes in it . . . I just had two more fuel lines to put on, the final steps, and there's an elbow connector coming out of the rebuilt injector pump that went into a coupling that goes up vertically that brought fuel from the primer pump to the injector pump and also fuel to the injectors—it came up to a T—when I was twisting the coupling into the injector pump, threading it into the injector pump, it broke off."

It was a four-dollar piece. On back order till May.

Once we moved out to Monroe Harbor, it would be a month of starting the generator with ether, or no power at all.

Providence has a way of lending a hand. Mark came home from the post office one night with a wonderful letter in his hand. "We're in!" he proclaimed. "We're at Belmont Harbor for the summer!" True, it was A Dock—known as the armpit of Belmont Harbor, tucked into the far north corner, closest to the bike path, and Lake Shore Drive, where all the debris from the harbor washes up, and people are literally right outside your door. But it was a dock, and shore power, and it meant we'd be spending the summer in beautiful Lincoln Park. No tender, no rowing, no swinging around a can in rough weather, and no lack of shore power or fresh water.

In July, Mark went to Orlando for a six-day professional conference. Usually, I liked to go with him on business; I worked on my laptop poolside, and I got to enjoy the rare luxury of a bathtub. But there were three reasons I didn't go with him: Florida—July—Disney.

Mark joked to his colleagues, "My wife's home, keeping the boat afloat."

Before he left, I fretted just a bit. For six days and five nights, I would be in charge of *Mazurka*. If something went wrong, I was the point person. This scared the hell out of me. It wasn't like the captain was backpacking in the Andes and unreachable, and not like he didn't leave me with a boat in working order—the water tanks were filled, the sewage was empty. In fact, everything on *Mazurka* was shipshape, part of Mark's plan to abstain from any work on the boat during the month of July. (If you own a boat, you are laughing hysterically right now.) And except for the first few days of the month, when the varnishing project went a little long, he kept his pledge.

Still, I didn't know a whole lot about this thing I lived on. Even after almost a year, when bells and whistles went off and stuff started happening for no reason, my first reaction was to ignore it till Mark fixed it. My knowledge ended at differentiating the flat-head screwdriver from the Phillips, and sometimes I didn't even do that.

I still regarded the boat as Mark's hobby, not mine, which released me from any major responsibility beyond the normal upkeep necessary to live anywhere. He'd lived on it long before I ever came into the picture. Without him, I can honestly say I would have never, ever moved onto a boat. In contrast, he loved it. There were few things that gave him as much joy and peace of mind as pulling apart the entire boat and putting it all back together. This was not my idea of fun. And since he regarded the work as fun, I stayed away from the work. I washed the dishes, did the laundry, scrubbed the floors and watered the plants and changed the litter box. Of the particular marine chores, I filled the water tanks, since that didn't require much effort beyond putting the hose in the tank and turning the water on, and it was clean. I reluctantly went to the pumpout dock, only because this job required two people; I tied up and scrubbed the toilets while Mark wielded the nasty pumpout hose.

I avoided anything having to do with repair, maintenance, or the engine room: three common terms aboard a boat.

While Mark sat in air-conditioned Orlando hotel conference rooms, *Mazurka* stayed afloat under my own "bachin' it" rhythm. I happily spent afternoons working at the table in the salon; I hung out on the aft deck, talking on my cell phone, grilling dinner. All around me, bikers biked, runners ran, dog walkers canoodled, drivers sped up LSD. Chicago basked in summertime. I liked living on a boat in the middle of it all. I felt like I owned the park.

Mark would call me in the evenings, telling me that I had made the right decision to stay home, that Disney was everywhere; no one said good-bye, they said, "Have a magical day!"

Our neighbors aboard the *Harbor Dog*, Steve and Cindy, kept an eye on me, knowing that I would be alone for the first time in our married life. Not like I hadn't been alone before. But it's different when you live on a boat.

I chatted them up dockside while I watered my containers of tomato plants and basil and they stooped over a sewing machine on their aft deck, yards and yards of beige canvas trailing out on the dock. They had made boating their family recreation, taking their two teenage kids on Lake Michigan trips, spending weekends in harbors. The boat was *both* their decision, and they shared the work together. That summer, they worked diligently to recanvas their boat. This is no small task, requiring them to manipulate measurements and corral canvas to sew covers for the windows and side railings. They hauled out the sewing machine and worked closely together, solving problems like how to make hundreds of holes for the grommets. (Soldering gun.)

I watched this togetherness closely, and began to feel pangs of guilt that while Mark had persevered through last year's varnishing in the hot sun, I had stayed in the air-conditioned cabin. True, this was his first love, long before I ever came into the picture. But I had agreed to live aboard, and in doing so had signed up for the work, too.

Beyond the guilt, beyond my slow maturing into "wife" and the recognition that marriage is about working together, something else was changing in me. I was getting to know *Mazurka*. I felt a kinship with her after the long winter, sitting with her in the frozen ice, doing everything we could to keep her warm and unlock the ice from her hull. We had really endured an ordeal, the three of us, and she hung in there. She never gave up, never complained, never resented us for forcing her to spend the winter in water. When we pushed off the ledge at River City for summer on Lake Michigan, she seemed as happy as we were to shake off the ropes and float free, cleaving the water as she was intended. *Mazurka* had her own personality— sturdy, slow, determined. She was never intimidated by the showy powerboats, and always befriended the ducks and dinghies. She knew her top speed was eight knots and, like the turtle who won the race, never pretended to be something else. Maybe her confidence came from knowing how much she was loved.

Not to say that I loved her—not quite, not yet. But I was coming to tolerate her, even respect her, with the quiet surrender of a woman who understands that her husband's first love has something to offer him that she cannot.

OUT OF GAS

One of the few movies Mark had on board (we didn't have a TV—
we watched movies on our laptops) was *White Squall*, a film about a
sailing ship with a crew of teenage boys captained by Jeff Bridges.
They encounter a huge storm at sea and some of the crew die, including the captain's wife. This movie was very vivid in my mind.

We watched it at the onset of our first full summer aboard together
as husband and wife when, as promised, we planned to travel Lake
Michigan. Our first trip would be a five-day Father's Day fishing

excursion with my parents. We were heading across the lake to South Haven, Michigan. Our preparations prompted questions from me, such as, "If we start to sink, how soon until we know? Will we have enough time to blow up the Zodiac?"

I wanted the reassurance that, in an emergency, I would know what to do and how to help everyone else aboard. So that I could remain calm, the captain could remain calm, and nobody else would freak out as we put on life vests and jumped into the Zodiac and fired off flares. My other concern was that we save our feline crewmates, and putting them in the Zodiac seemed the best option.

Off the coast of Chicago, the concern was not so great, as the playpen area in front of the John Hancock, for instance, was only about twelve feet deep. If we started to sink, we would just bring everybody up to the flybridge, put on life jackets, and wait for the Coast Guard, who would probably arrive before the water even reached our feet.

We came up with a plan in case of emergency while under way: Put on life jackets, radio the Coast Guard our coordinates, blow up the Zodiac, hop in, fire off flares, wait. Mark bought a new DSC radio that would broadcast our GPS coordinates to the Coast Guard if we activated it. (I suspected this purchase was made more because it was a cool gadget than any actual need.)

Under way, the only way to tell that we were sinking was if we actually ran into something and started to visibly take on water. "The real threat is that we would sink at the dock," Mark said, describing the six places water can get into the boat: hull fittings at both toilets, the propeller drive shaft, heater intake, engine intake, and generator intake.

It's estimated that, for every boat that sinks while under way, there are four boats that sink while tied to the dock. Recreational boats spend a lot more time at the dock than under way, a lot more time untended by captains, and things like a rotten bilge pump or a weak battery can lead to a boat sinking, even in relatively shallow water.

A few days before we left, oddly enough, *Mazurka's* alarm system called Mark's phone while he was at work. He called the harbor office, and they did a quick check: There was water leaking inside. Mark sped home to find an inch of water in the salon. The drinking water filter beneath the sink had burst (which he had just fixed the weekend prior with super-duper glue; "That's not going to leak anymore," he said), and the line was leaking water everywhere. He shut off the water, mopped it up, and returned to work, very upset.

It took a couple days to get the right piece to fix the line. In the meantime, we collected water at the dockside spigot. We kept *Mazurka's* water off, except when washing dishes and showering, and then we kept a bucket under the sink to collect the runoff.

Adapt, overcome, improvise.

My parents were ideal guests to travel with by boat. Our childhood summers were spent camping in a twenty-four-foot Coachman trailer on the backwaters of the Mississippi, my dad and brother fishing for crappie and walleye. My parents loved water, they loved to fish, and they weren't afraid of bunking up in tight spaces.

The night before we left for South Haven, we dropped anchor in front of the John Hancock building, thinking it would be fun to sleep downtown and watch the sunrise as we cruised to South Haven in the morning. We cleaned up the kitchen, turned out the lights, hunkered down, and then . . .

Slosh slosh slosh—a moment of calm—slosh slosh slosh—clang clang clang—clinking of glasses in the cupboards as they were thrown side-to-side—moment of calm—slosh slosh slosh . . .

I would fall asleep for the still moment, only to be jerked awake by the next hit. It wasn't the calm, soothing rocking of the rolling seas; it was a downright assault.

"I don't think I can sleep like this," I told Mark.

"Me neither."

Slosh slosh slosh.

"Are my parents asleep?"

"I think so."

Clang clang clang.

"We're getting echo waves off shore," Mark said.

Slosh slosh slosh.

"Do you want to go back to Belmont Harbor?" he asked.

"No. It's too much trouble. If my parents are sleeping, I can get through it, too."

"I'll go start the engine. You stay here."

I lay in bed—slosh slosh slosh—clang clang clang—calm—slosh slosh slosh—as Mark started up the engine. I heard Dad go up top and the two of them pulling up the anchor. I was so tired I didn't even get up to help. We rocked our way back to Belmont Harbor, and the last thing I remember was the sudden stillness of being tied to the dock, and then sleep.

The next morning, the sun was high over the horizon by the time we got up. "I've never been so glad as when I heard Mark start that engine," my mom told us while the coffee brewed. "I thought for sure I was going to upchuck." Mark and Dad relayed the madness that went on while the two of us stayed in bed: the coolers being thrown from side to side, and both of them crawling across the deck so as not to lose their balance.

Nobody was earning any badges for enduring unnecessary hardship on this excursion. By ten o'clock, we were cruising across calm waters to South Haven.

We arrived just as the marina office was closing up for the night. They assigned us a slip alongside the sailboats rather than the powerboats. "Those guys like us," Mark said, maneuvering into the dock. "We're not that far from a sailboat. They're all thinking about trawlers, anyway."

I let Hunter and Leo roam around on the dock, taking their tour of boats. One by one, they would board each boat, wander around the deck, then move on to the next. Leo found a sailboat that was open (the owners were at dinner) and disappeared inside for nearly an hour. I could see him through the top hatch, sniffing everything. There's only a slight problem that I can't board the boats my cats feel more than welcome to explore—I stand on the dock, calling to them, shaking their treat can, utterly ignored.

The next night, after a fruitless search for salmon and perch—"Is anybody catching anything out there?" our fellow fishermen called helplessly on the radio—we docked and had dinner after sunset.

As dusk fell, the sailors emerged from their hatches, curious about *Mazurka*, confessing they'd always wanted a trawler. They could barely contain their excitement when Mark offered a tour. With everyone crammed into the salon, he told tales of previous mishaps. "And here's the engine room, the battery chargers . . . you know, I made an expensive mistake with those battery chargers. I thought they weren't charging my batteries—I thought the batteries were dead—I went through three new batteries before I realized I had to turn the damn thing on . . ." (The story of owning a boat, truly, is narrated by all the things that have gone wrong with it.) They all laughed, then told their own battery charger stories, leaving them off so the refrigerator was not powered, the sump pump not powered, the batteries drained so low they had to rush out and buy distilled water.

My mom, sitting beside me in her pajamas, waiting for them to leave as it was nearly midnight, turned to me and said, "I have no idea what they're talking about, do you?"

"Sort of," I said. "I lived through it."

But I could only tell certain things about it. I couldn't articulate the power of the generator, or which wire went where, or even where the battery charger was and which of the countless Where's-Waldo items down there were the batteries. I was just not that interested. But I could tell you what it was like to watch Mark try to coordinate hauling three 80-pound batteries from Monroe Street into the tender boat and onto *Mazurka* in the pinpointing heat of late July.

It grated me, just a bit, that I fit into the gender stereotype of the wife who didn't know nothing about those li'l electronic thingies. My training in that area ended in junior high when I built a pencil holder and earned an A in shop class. I was sure I could learn, if I got a manual and muddled my way through it. Which is exactly what Mark and all these other boaters did—they kept making mistakes till one of the mistakes was right, and then they learned how to do it. Then they could tell fellow boaters about the time they turned the battery charger off and the wife was upset because she had no refrigeration on board.

"Oh, you mean your husband's boat," is what the Westrec guy had said to me when I called about the money they were trying to squeeze out of us. I bristled but let it go, though I wanted to say something like, *No, my boat—I live here, too.* And I supposed in some matrimonial sense it was my boat, but really, I was reminded once again that I never would live aboard were it not for Mark.

It's kind of weird to let somebody else be responsible for your good time. Maybe that's a good question to consider about the person you want to marry. If you relinquished control and let them be responsible for your good time, would they make sure you had fun? And could you do the same?

After three days and no fish, we headed back to Chicago early on the morning of Father's Day. Somewhere off the shore of Michigan we hit a pocket where the high- and low-pressure systems met: This was where blackflies hide. *Mazurka* was overcome with thousands of flies of all natures—tiger and leopard print, big and small, fast and slow, all of them biting. They were everywhere, dying by the hundreds, feasting on one another's carcasses and on us. We rinsed the boat again and again to no avail. No insect repellent or thick clothing could hold them off. Finally, we admitted defeat and hid inside. Mark cleared off the mail stack from the helm and piloted the boat from the cabin. We tucked towels into every crevice. In relief, we only had to swat one or two at a time, rather than hundreds.

I was still coming out of a hangover, feeling stupid and ashamed for drinking all the liquor (and having to go ashore for more) and picking a fight with Mark the day before. Things were coming to a head with my drinking. I knew I had to stop, and I knew I had to ask for help to do it.

When we were within an hour from shore, and could see the downtown skyline, we heard over Channel 16, "Mayday! Mayday!"

Mark turned it up; we leaned in closer.

The Coast Guard out of Monroe Harbor responded, asking for the nature of the problem.

"I'm stuck," the guy replied.

"What do you mean, you're stuck?" the Coast Guard answered.

There was no response. The Coast Guard called for them repeatedly. No response. Finally, the boater called again, "Mayday! Mayday! I'm stuck!"

The Coast Guard answered again, asking for the location and nature of the problem.

"I'm off Fullerton Harbor," the boater said (there is no Fullerton Harbor, but we imagine he was somewhere just north of downtown). "The engine just shut off. I tried to get it going, but it won't start. I'm stuck."

"Are you taking on any water?" the Coast Guard asked.

"Negative."

The Coast Guard then asked the boater to switch to a different channel. We switched along with them.

"First time in my life I ever heard somebody call mayday," Dad said.

On Channel 22, the boater described how he couldn't start the engine, and he was afraid to try—he feared taking in air. At that point, the Coast Guard asked him for his cell phone number so they could call him privately.

But we knew the rest of the story. He ran out of gas.

"Who runs out of gas on the lake?" Dad asked.

I looked at the captain. "I'm sure no one on this boat."

It's never a good sign on a first date to run out of gas—especially if your mode of transportation is a boat.

A few years before I met him, Mark's first-grade teacher, Sister Susan, set him up on a blind date with a woman who lives in Milwaukee. Mark lived in Chicago at the time (on land), and decided it would be fun to take his boat, the *Escape Hatch*, up to Milwaukee for the blind date. But it was a much longer ride than he anticipated, and by the time he got within a quarter mile of shore . . . he ran out of gas.

He had to call the Coast Guard to help him, which is no small thing. They board your boat, check out every nook and cranny, charge you for the gas and their time, and no doubt give you a lot of shit for being a dumb ass who ran out of gas. All the time this was happening, Mark could see his blind date sitting on the dock, waiting for him.

Needless to say, they didn't hit it off. Not that they didn't get along, there just wasn't a spark.

As a parting gift, he sent her a kite. I scoffed when he told me that detail. "What?" he said. "We talked about kite flying."

Not long after our South Haven adventure, on a beautiful summer Sunday afternoon, I had eight hours of work to do for a deadline that was about a dozen monkeys on my back. Instead, I blew it off because it was just too damn nice outside. Beautiful summer Sunday afternoons don't happen all that often in Chicago. Blessed with blue skies and calm waters and a sweet breeze, I felt it a crime to refuse the gift.

Rather than taking out *Mazurka*, we decided to go for a ride in the little Zodiac, which we christened "Li'l Chopin." We loaded up with towels and sunscreen and soda and headed for Montrose Harbor, about three miles north . . . maybe a little more. On the way out there, I asked Mark, "How much gas does that thing hold?"

"Enough to get us there and back," he assured me. "I just filled it up."

We motored for nearly an hour before reaching Montrose Beach, where we put down the anchor just outside the buoys. The beach was filled with people, with boaters and Jet Skiers and kayakers not far from us. The water was warm, and we swam around the Zodiac for a long time before deciding to jump back in and head home. Except you can't really jump into a Zodiac. Or climb. Or gracefully lumber up. A Zodiac raft is damn near impossible to climb into if you're in the water. Mark and I tried to climb up on opposite sides, to steady the boat, but as he was trying to pull a leg up, I was laughing hysterically. He had one leg in the air as a boat motored by. "Need some help?" they called. Mark gazed nonchalantly at them over his leg. "No, we're fine." We tried climbing up the stern, bracing against the motor. Finally, we tried the old-fashioned way: I climbed up on Mark, into the Zodiac, and pulled him up after me.

I was driving back to Belmont, with Mark in the front, when about a quarter of the way into the trip . . . put . . . put . . . put. We were out of gas.

"Well, I kind of just filled it up," Mark explained. "When we were in South Haven. Maybe it was halfway full."

We had a long way to row. Like, almost three miles. Mark took the oars, and I began bailing the boat with a pop can (water had collected from waves over the bow). Lesson for next time: Bring extra gas and a bucket.

This would take hours. We started bickering about the best way to get back. I voted that we row to shore and guide the Zodiac in the water from shore, via rope. Mark thought it best to row all the way back to *Mazurka*. "I just hope the oars don't break," he said.

Just then—I'm not kidding—the piece that attached the plastic oar to the raft cracked, making it impossible to row.

Luckily, we had extra supplies in the emergency bag, including the plastic piece that cracked. We were putting it together when a Jet Ski sidled up beside us. "Need some help?" asked the driver, his arms covered in tattoos.

Our new friend Dan took our rope and towed us back to Belmont, very slowly. Mark looked back to me, his brow furrowed, "The only thing I'm worried about . . ."

"Don't say it!" I yelled. "Don't say it!"

He didn't say it—not till Dan dropped us off just inside Belmont Harbor, and Mark was rowing us back to *Mazurka*. "The only thing I was worried about is that you're not supposed to tow a Zodiac. The ropes are only secured to the raft with glue. They could rip right off and the Zodiac would sink."

Duly noted, Captain.

Within minutes of arriving home, Mark fashioned a makeshift ladder for the small raft.

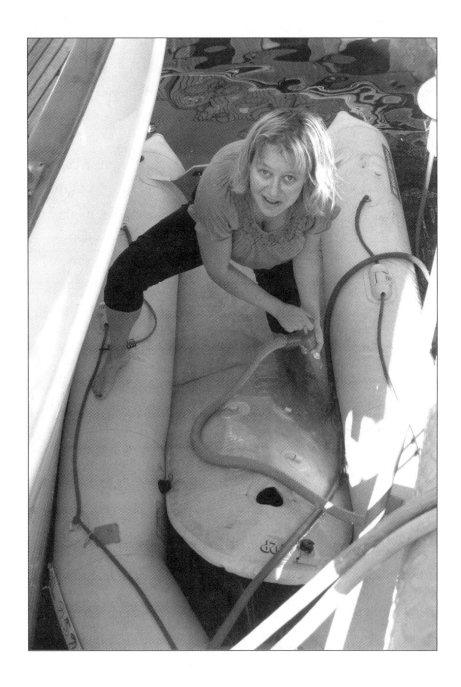

A BOAT FROM TEMPERANCE

Vessel names tell you a lot about the captain, a lot about the boat.

There are the usuals: *Princess*, *Star Gazer*, and all manner of women's names.

There are variations on a theme: *Fan-a-Sea*, *Fan-t-Sea*; *Missed Opportunity*, *Mist Opportunity*.

There are names that make you wonder if the captain ever considered the fact that he would have to announce his vessel to harbors, lock systems, and the U.S. Coast Guard in an emergency. There's the *Triple Nipple*, *Honey I Shrunk My Wallet*, and our favorite: *Turd Cutter*.

The name *Mazurka* is the unintended present of the previous owner, who wanted to take the name with him after he sold the boat. Mark refused. Normally, a new captain will rename his boat with an elaborate ceremony. Mark kept things as is.

A mazurka is a Polish folk dance in triple meter with a lively tempo and a heavy accent on the second or third beat, popular for dancing.

Chopin composed fifty-one mazurkas for solo piano. Musicians and Poles know what a mazurka is. Moored in Chicago, the city with the world's second largest population of Polish people (just after Warsaw), we often had boaters and civilians call to us in Polish. We shrugged and shook our heads.

Like the name of the boat, Mark had never bothered to change the city of origin that appears under the name.

One early morning at the pumpout dock, I was standing at the stern looking everything over when the home port of *Mazurka* caught my eye. "Temperance, MI," it read.

"Hey Mark," I called, "This is a temperance boat."

Temperance, a small town in the lower southeast corner of Michigan, close to Toledo and Lake Erie, is a long way from Chicago. You could drive there in about four and a half hours. By boat, by *Mazurka* that goes eight miles top speed, it would take two weeks, up and around the mitten of Michigan.

Whenever we pulled into a transient slip, boaters assumed with admiration that we had made the long trip from Temperance. Some people wondered if we were making the Great Loop, the long journey circling through the waterways of eastern North America, including the Great Lakes.

"No," Mark would tell them, "I just never changed the boat's name when I bought it."

"Oh, good grief," said one of our Waukegan neighbors.

Random House Webster's College Dictionary defines *temperance* as: 1. Moderation or self-restraint; self-control. 2. Habitual moderation in any indulgence, appetite, etc. 3. Total abstinence from alcoholic liquors.

I like this three-part definition, because it pretty much sums up in chronological order how I drank. I started moderately, with whiskey and wine, proceeded to habitual moderation, in that I made it a habit to drink often (moderation is up for debate), and finally, at the age of thirty-two, fully aware that I was a full-blown alcoholic with little to no chance of ever stopping on my own, I gave up the ship, so to speak, and the booze.

It's completely ridiculous to think that I could ever moderate any-thing—particularly alcohol.

After a brief summer of not drinking following my tearful Sun-day-morning confession to the anonymous priest, I resumed "casual" drinking sometime around our wedding. Although Mark did drink—and was often around people who drank—he never actually drank that much. One beer was more than plenty. Leaving me to wonder, when were we going to get good and drunk? The answer, apparently, was never. So for our first months as newlyweds, we drank a glass of wine every day. Maybe two.

The attempt to control my drinking was excruciating.

My drinking came up a few times while we dated. Once, Mark called me at my apartment. "Why are there all these empty bottles on my shelf?" I knew exactly why they were there. When he was away and I hung out alone on his boat, I had drunk up a lot of his liquor. Worried what he would say if he noticed a bunch of bottles missing (and know-ing he wouldn't touch them on his own), I left the empty bottles on the shelf. On the phone, I didn't confess this. I said something about him making me feel guilty for drinking, and he dropped the subject.

On another occasion, I had gotten drunk quickly at a party and started badgering him for not paying me enough attention. He said he would drive me home, and I got belligerent. He shrugged with indifference and dropped me off at my apartment.

Later, he said things like, "I just need to take care of myself." I had no idea what he meant.

About four months into our marriage, I told Mark I wanted to quit my day job and pursue my dream of writing full-time. Mark is an exceptionally kind, generous person, who wanted me to be happy, who wanted to do whatever he could to help me achieve my dream. He said, "Of course." By February, I had become a full-time freelance writer.

Without my realizing it, my daily life soon became a habit of hiding how much I drank. On days I was working from home, I would start drinking between 3 and 4 p.m. Afternoons were dangerous times for me—if I was home alone, the agitation of the day would build, and by afternoon I would start looking for relief. I would pour one glass of wine and tell myself, "That's all I'll be having." But before that first glass was even half gone, I was itching for the next one.

Then there was the trick of getting drunk, but not too drunk—just drunk enough to be buzzed but still able to hide it from Mark. About half an hour before he came home, I would stop drinking, eat something, brush my teeth. After he arrived home, I had to get dinner on the table and make sure we sat down to eat as quickly as possible, so that I could open a bottle of wine with dinner and continue the buzz. While he sipped one glass like any normal person (my husband has the uncanny ability to actually leave some wine in the glass and walk away from the table—something I have never been able to comprehend, let alone do), I would suck down two glasses, then insist on cleaning up and shoo him from the salon so I could finish off the remaining wine in his glass and the rest of the bottle. And if he had something to do before dinner—if dinner was delayed even half an hour—I was certain that he was doing it on purpose, because he knew I wanted to drink, and he was trying to stop me.

On weekends it was worse. If we were both at home, I would sip from bottles of Haitian rum I had hidden around the boat. (On our way home from the medical mission, we had bought two cases of Haitian rum at the airport in Port-au-Prince. They were gifts. I was afraid that Mark was actually going to give them away, and stashed them all over the boat. But hide a bottle? Me? Never.) If Mark was out for the afternoon and I stayed home, I would feel the obligation to do things around the boat, get something accomplished, but I'd tell myself it would be that much more bearable with a glass of wine or rum and Coke or just straight whiskey. Just one, I would tell myself. And maybe I could keep it to that one, so tightly wound and determined not to have another one. Or I would take a few more sips. But more likely, that one would turn into two or three, and then, completely despondent and depressed, I'd go to bed for a nap, longing for the day and the weekend to be over so things could go back to "normal."

What normal was, I had long forgotten.

Without my really being conscious of it, my days were starting to revolve around when it was time to drink, and the need to hide it from everyone around me. Before I met Mark, I'd always hung out with men who drank like I did; how I drank wasn't unusual because that's what everybody was doing. Let me tell you, there's nothing like living with a normal drinker to really bring out the problem. I yearned for places where I could drink openly. And it was this impulse that, when we brought my parents on board for a Father's Day fishing excursion, led me to an all-out three-day drinking binge. I polished off the bottle of Ten High by the second day. I went into town to buy a bigger bottle, and a bottle of Bailey's, and the next morning at five while everyone else was fishing, I was pouring Bailey's into coffee, then pouring whiskey into everything. I was blitzed by

10 a.m., passed out with the spins by 1. I woke in the late afternoon as we pulled into port, half drunk and half hung over. My parents perhaps sensed trouble brewing and took a trip out in the Zodiac.

Alone in the salon, Mark told me, "I just don't like the drinking." Then he said the kicker:

"It makes me wonder about having kids."

"What?" I said defensively. "That their mother will be a drunk?"

"No," he said. "What they'll inherit."

This stopped me. This I could not argue. We both had alcoholism in our bloodlines. I knew I was alcoholic. I had known for some time, but didn't want to believe that being alcoholic meant I could no longer drink. Why not be a functional alcoholic? Except that I was no longer functioning. I knew I couldn't control it. And I wouldn't be able to control whether our children got it, either. The most I would be able to do would be to model for them what it was like to live as a sober alcoholic.

That night, Mark and I took a trip out in the Zodiac by ourselves. We passed by the concert on the riverfront, the many boats parked in front, people partying, and headed out to the lake to a secluded beach. It was the middle of June, and so close to the solstice, the lake was still illuminated by a line of dark pink shining up beyond the clouds. I stood in the cold water, and knew I had to stop drinking, and had to ask for help to do so. Neither of these did I want to do. But I had learned to let Mark into my world, and now it was time to let some others in, too.

The next day, Father's Day, as we cruised across Lake Michigan in the plague of swarming blackflies, I didn't drink. The following day, back in Chicago, I went up to the flybridge alone and made a phone call to ask for help. It was the first stride on a long road of recovery.

As days passed and the fog of alcohol began to clear, I slowly started walking through a day completely sober. I began to see how everything I did all day long had been attached to drinking. Agitation and anxiety—uncertainty about the future and what I was supposed to do—didn't go away. Emotions came down on me full-force, and I physically ached with the new experience of being "checked in" at all times. I had started drinking alcoholically after college to blunt my emotions, but after just a few years the blunting object became the only focus. My first question of the day had become, at what point today do I get to start drinking? And what do I need to do to make sure it happens? Often it wasn't even planned—it was just what I did.

But now, getting through a day without alcohol took a lot of planning. Sobriety—real sobriety, not just swearing off alcohol—demanded constant vigilance and work to learn the tools I would need to stay sober. For the first time as an adult, I was learning to be a full participant in life.

Mark supported anything I said I needed to do to learn this new way of life. He wasn't surprised to hear me say I was an alcoholic, and he didn't try to control my recovery. Instead, as he told me before, he took care of himself.

Though one night he confessed, "I knew there was something wrong in our marriage. I just thought the problem was me."

That summer, I was too embarrassed to tell people I had stopped drinking and they shouldn't bring wine on board, so I said nothing and guests kept bringing wine. One night, about a month into sobriety, out in the middle of Lake Michigan, somebody stuck a full goblet of red wine right under my nose. "You gotta try this," she said. The smell went right into me, igniting my whole face. I squirmed away and escaped to the tiny head. I was trapped; I couldn't leave the boat, there was no cell phone reception for me to make a call. There was just enough room in that bathroom for me to get down on my knees, and I prayed: "God, I don't want to drink today. Please help me." Then I went back to my hosting duties. The party went on for several more hours. People drank, sure, but not me. I wasn't even fighting it. The compulsion was just gone.

When we returned to A Dock, after our guests had gone, I looked at the shelf to see eight bottles of red wine staring back at me. I had never had eight bottles of wine in my house—*ever*. I had fantasized about having a full wine cellar, sure; but if there was one, I drank it.

Eight bottles.

I turned to my husband. "Can you give some of this away?"

So Mark started up and down A Dock, not finding it too difficult to give away Malbec and Cabernet and Shiraz to our fellow boaters. I'm sure he became everybody's new best friend that night.

On A Dock alone, there was *Absolute and Cranberry*, *Rolling Rock II* (in a green font just like the label), *Bumpy Night* (flanked by two martini glasses), and *Aquaholics*. Somewhere in Chicago, *Ship Faced* and *Betty Ford* cruised. That was cool.

Me? I started living on a boat from Temperance.

THE VIEW FROM OUR FRONT DOOR

I have to tell Mark he's not a bachelor and he can't do this anymore was my first thought on a hot and stormy July Sunday morning, waking at 4 a.m. to pouring rain and Mark and Carl discussing the air conditioner.

I called out to them, "You guys aren't seriously fixing the air conditioner now, are you?"

No, not fixing the air conditioner; preparing to go fishing. I remembered that I had agreed to this early-morning trip. Not because

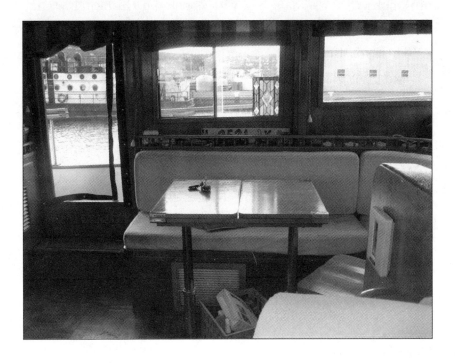

I like getting up that early, or because I'm wild about fishing. But I liked the crew, Jeff and Carl, and it seemed a sin, at least in my family, to not go out early-morning fishing if you live on a boat.

Jeff arrived shortly, telling tales of the strange activity you see in Chicago alleys at four thirty in the morning.

At five thirty we were headed out at sixty degrees, watching the downtown skyscrapers shrink to chess pieces. Sears Tower was the king, 900 North Michigan the queen, and Hancock the rook.

In an hour we reached a ledge that dropped from seventy-five to one hundred feet deep, and they cast their lines. Half the sky was rainy, the other half sunny. We had calm waters. And not much happening.

I had little patience for fishing, unless they were biting. As a kid I would bring a book with me when I went out in the boat with my dad, or ice skates along in the winter. But fishing from my house, things were different. I made everybody breakfast, did some work, cleaned up. I took a chair out to the bow with a book and a blanket. It was the first time I had ever been surrounded by 360 degrees of water.

When you free yourself from the constraints of land, you free yourself from all the landlocked worries: bills and schedules and obligations and all the other daily to-do tasks that weigh us down. When you're surrounded by water, you're alone, and also acutely aware that you're part of something much bigger.

After nearly a year on board, there was still so much about this boat I didn't know. It was full of surprises, things I never expected— like the view from our front door.

You never know what you might see outside your front door when you live on a boat. One winter day I came home for lunch and while making a salad, I caught sight of somebody's legs outside the front

door on the dock.

I took a closer look: white guy, mid-forties, balding, looking around. This was not unusual. People came out all the time to take pictures of the Loop or get a view of the river.

But the next thing I knew he was unzipping his jeans.

I opened the door and yelled, "Hey!" catching him mid-piss, a yellow puddle collecting in the snow right outside our door.

He jumped and put it away and ran off. As he was hightailing it down the dock, I heard him call to one of our neighbors, "I thought you were the only one out here!"

On a summer weeknight in Lincoln Park, I was eating dinner alone in the salon when I looked out our front door and spied a woman sitting supine on a tree stump, arms back, one knee up, wearing a long necklace, and a man taking her photo.

I looked again: Yep, she was naked.

Partly because I was sure no one would believe me (Mark was gone for the night), and partly because I couldn't believe it, I grabbed my digital camera and started shooting photos of the photo shoot.

Suddenly the photographer wrapped his leather jacket around the woman and they got into a parked car. A car drove by. When the coast was clear, the photographer and model returned, finished the shoot, and drove away.

The next day, the city came and cut down the tree stump.

(Which led me to a theory that this was a top-secret ritual for Chicago tree stumps about to become sawdust. Somewhere in the depths of the City Streets and Sanitation offices, there was a huge wall with hundreds of photos of naked women posed on stumps.)

When your front door is on water, there are certain risks to avoid when coming home.

Every time I climbed aboard *Mazurka*, I clutched everything tightly to me—keys, phone, laptop, wallet—because the inevitable could always happen, when making the leap from pier to deck; in the deceptively short six inches of just-a-step, you could lose what you needed most.

In a year of living aboard, this had not yet happened to me.

Nor had it happened to Mark, which was somewhat surprising because he had a tendency to lose almost everything. Until one morning when he was on deck, tying up an extra fender and somehow, as he leaned over the railing, the rail knocked into the cell phone holstered to his belt; the phone went flying into the air and landed with a plop in the water.

He came racing into the cabin. "I dropped my phone in the water. Oh my God, I'm sick about it. It had my whole calendar. I haven't synced it in months."

I thought of stories I had heard of people dropping cell phones in stranger places—like latrines in India—retrieving the phone, letting it dry, and finding it worked good as new. I had the same experience when my phone was caught in the rain. After a day of buzzing, it dried out and I was able to use it. I reassured my husband. "We can get it."

The lucky thing about mooring on A Dock is that the water is less than six feet deep. Below us, thanks to the work of invasive zebra mussels, we could often see the bottom. While the salmon fishermen watched us from across the harbor, we attempted to shield the sun so we could see to the bottom—no luck.

"I'm just sick about it," Mark kept repeating.

"Try the net," I said.

"But what will that do?" he asked. "I can't even see it."

"Try dredging the bottom," I suggested, "right where you dropped it."

Against his better judgment, he did as I advised. One sweep, nothing. The second sweep, and up came the cell phone. We erupted into cheers, causing the fishermen across the way to wonder if we'd come upon a new method for catching salmon.

I wish I could tell you that in twenty-four hours the phone was good as new. This was not the case. All of Mark's information was gone forever to the bottom of Belmont Harbor.

Anything—or anyone—can easily fall in when your front door is on the water.

One night I was watering our garden (six tomato plants, basil, sage, dill, parsley, cilantro, and chives all lining the dock) when something resembling a small shark swam beneath me, between the dock and the boat. I looked down, thinking it was a large carp. But it was hairy, and swimming above water. And there were two.

A few nights earlier one of our Venetian Night guests told us she saw something strange swimming in the water. "Not a raccoon," she said, "not a rat, not a beaver—but like a beaver—they have them at the Shedd Aquarium."

"An otter?" I asked.

"Yeah! An otter!" she said. We all told her there was no way there were any otters living in Belmont Harbor. But that's what they looked like to me, swimming below my garden.

The security guard came by. "What are those things?" I asked her.

"Ducks," she said, smoking a cigarette, not looking where I was pointing.

"No," I told her, "*those* things."

"Oh my God . . ." She stared, cigarette dangling from her lip.

We stood together for a long time, watching the "otters," trying to convince ourselves maybe they were beavers. Furry, long, with narrow heads and small teeth. (I learned later they were muskrats.)

We walked with them as they swam back along the boats. I stopped in front of *Mazurka* and picked up the hose to finish watering the plants. Hunter and Leo had come out by that time and were roaming around. "Don't you worry about those cats?" the security guard asked me. "That they might fall in?"

"No," I told her. "They've lived on the boat for a year—they're pretty agile."

Cats falling in the drink was an early concern. I knew from childhood (and cruel boys throwing cats in the Mississippi River) that cats are good swimmers. Mark and I had a rough plan that if one fell in, we'd throw him a line or a hook or get the net or steer him toward the swim deck, then scrub him clean.

I finished watering the plants and took my bags inside and came back out in pursuit of Leo, who was making his way down the dock. The last I saw of Hunter—who is unfortunately the clumsy one— he was standing on the *Harbor Dog*, ready to jump to the *Mazurka*.

The next thing I heard was Hunter's claws scrape the side of the boat. I turned just in time to see him miss one of the ropes and land in the water. He could swim all right, but he also cried like you've never heard a drowning cat cry in your life. I screamed for Mark— who was on the phone inside—and rapped at the door for him while running to get a hook.

Hunter was swimming in circles and crying and gurgling water. I had half a mind to jump in for him, right where the muskrats had been. I extended one of the hooks into the water, and Hunter grabbed on, but as I lifted him out he fell back into the water. I screamed again for Mark and threw Hunter a rope (who knows what I expected him to do with the rope). He was trying to climb up the flat walls, slowly swimming toward a nearby swim deck, still crying, still gurgling water.

Just then, Mark emerged with the giant fishing net (it was hidden at the bottom of the lazarette, the storage area at the stern). In one swoop he fished out the poor cat. Hunter stumbled around a bit, then let me pick him up and take him inside and rinse him in the shower.

That answered that question.

(Months later, when we were staying on G Dock, Leo had his turn in the water. Mark and I were locking up to leave the boat and round-ing up the cats—Hunter was inside, but Leo was nowhere. We heard meowing out on the dock, but couldn't see him anywhere. I knelt down and looked under the dock; there was Leo, sitting on the float, soaking wet. I jumped in and he willingly let me pick him up and drag him through the water. As soon as his paws hit the dock he raced for *Mazurka*, straight to the litter box to hide. We were combing clay litter out of wet cat hair for a long time.)

One of the best parts of living on a boat is that you can change the view from your front door whenever the spirit moves you. I soon learned that subzero nights and a freezing river are bearable penance for all that summer has to offer the liveaboard.

On a Thursday night, when we wanted to go out to dinner, we

started up the engine and drove our house out to a new view of the city. We were the only folks out there in the playpen, and we dropped anchor and grilled dinner, watching Venus shine brightly in the west. Hunter and Leo came out on deck and wandered around.

Rinsing the lettuce before dinner, I heard something new. "What's that sound?" I asked Mark. It was all about sounds and smells aboard a boat. Smells differentiated between leaking fuel and gray water that's overflowed and sewage in the bilge. Sounds differentiated between a sump pump working properly and a water pump that won't shut off—which is what I was hearing—which indicated that the water tanks were empty. Sure enough, mid-sentence, the faucet ran dry.

"Looks like we're out of water."

We were never too far from the next chore, the next potential problem.

Surrounded by water yet out of water, empty tanks were not an emergency—not when dinner was grilling and the night was still. So we sat on the aft cabin and ate perch and zucchini with our fingers, watching the traffic on Lake Shore Drive, and the darkening rooftops of skyscrapers. And in a while we hauled up the anchor, cruised back to Belmont, and filled up the water tanks at the slip. Then I took a shower, just because I could.

We planned a long weekend trip up the western coast of Lake Michigan, and to kick it off we invited twenty people aboard for an evening of dinner and fireworks.

In his bachelor days, Mark threw a lot of parties on *Mazurka*. He believed having a boat in Chicago meant taking people out to show them a rare view of the city. He also entertained like a bachelor— meaning there wasn't a whole lot of cleanup before the party, or a whole lot of preparation at all. (I should have known this by his casual attitude and bedlam of tools the first night I came aboard *Mazurka*.) A cooler full of beer and some brats for the grill was plenty. Actually, Mark was a very good cook and made sure his guests ate well. Still, his lack of anxiety before a party made me even more anxious. Didn't we have to deep-clean the boat and prepare a seven-course meal and get a haircut?

For parties on a boat, the answer is no.

Jay Gatsby threw all his amazing parties for one reason—to get his lost love Daisy to attend. So he never really mingled at his parties; he would linger on the outskirts, scanning the guests for a glimpse of his true love.

On *Mazurka*, Gatsby would have nowhere to hide.

We always brought people together for different reasons—colleagues, or family, or friends who really should meet each other. Mark auctioned off a boat ride for a student fund-raiser at his university. Sometimes they were guests neither of us had met—a friend visiting from out of town would bring along their family who lived in the suburbs.

You can learn a lot about people by cruising around with them. The group dynamics were fascinating. We would take a group of people who perhaps had never met and throw them all together on a boat. We'd stick a life jacket on them and tell them hold on to the rope as we passed through the locks. Suddenly everyone was a lifelong friend.

Whatever judgments you make of someone in the first five minutes will disappear once you set out. You're on the water, where anything can happen. The crew is all you have to depend on. Dormant parts of a personality suddenly come alive on rocky waters; someone you thought was wishy-washy, or shy, suddenly emerges with strong, deft decision making. The introvert can lead the crew; the know-it-all sulks in the cabin. The way a person reacts to the beautiful lake, or challenging weather, or the immense space says a lot about them. And nearly every single time we arrived back at port, our guests would exchange phone numbers and emails. They were a cohesive crew.

So taking my cue from the calm captain, I learned to relax and enjoy the party going on at my front door. I learned not to apologize for the diesel smell. (Or any other strange smells. It was a boat; there was nothing we could do.) We always gave a tour to our guests, making sure to emphasize how the plumbing worked. In rough water, I would allay people's fears by telling them what the captain had told me: There was no way this boat was going to tip over. I learned to tell guests to bring a dish to share, and I learned to let people help clean up. I was amazed at the organization skills of our guests. We were barely done tying up at the dock when the flybridge would be clean and people were hauling out garbage bags.

Experience had taught us that twelve to fourteen guests were optimal for our boat. *Mazurka* could host up to thirty, but it was damn uncomfortable trying to squeeze through the walkways, and people would end up parking themselves in one spot all evening just because it was easier than trying to maneuver through crowds. A dozen people meant everybody could move about freely, mix and mingle, and even escape to a quiet area if they needed some alone time on the water.

Earlier in the season, we hosted my friend Kathy's thirtieth birthday party—probably thirty people in attendance that night, and *Mazurka* listed only a bit.

Before our long getaway weekend, when we planned to host

twenty as a going-away party before motoring our front door up the Wisconsin coast, a violent thunderstorm planted itself directly over *Mazurka* two hours before the guests were set to arrive. I sat atop the flybridge, the only place I could steal a WiFi signal, hunched over my laptop to protect it from the rain, emailing my guests to say that as the rain was coming sideways, we were probably going to cancel. But I didn't know for sure. It could pass and by 7 p.m. there might be beautiful, smooth sailing. At five thirty, I decided to cancel, and I called everyone to let them know. By six thirty? You guessed it—clear skies and calm water.

Mark and I headed out, just the two of us. We cruised up to the playpen and dropped anchor in front of the Hancock building. Our plan was to spend the night and in the morning make our way north, to Waukegan for a night, then on to Milwaukee for a long weekend.

It's a cool thing to be able to make a decision to go on an extended trip, and half an hour later you're on your way. The feeling you may have forgotten something doesn't go away, but you have the peace of mind knowing that you couldn't possibly have forgotten anything: You're taking your whole house with you.

The playpen was calm, protected by breakwalls, except for powerboats passing through at top speed, sending ripples of high waves. We put out the stabilizer—a hinged wing of stainless steel that suspended down into the water from the boom; as the boat rocked, it floated up and down in the water, creating enough drag to keep us from rocking too much. It didn't completely take away the rocking, but it made it a whole lot more comfortable. The passing storm stirred the water and dropped the temperature, so it was too cold to swim. Instead we spent the evening on the aft deck, in a sleeping bag, drinking tea, watching the fireworks over Navy Pier.

Afterward, most of the boats left the playpen, except for two powerboats, rafted together for a party. Without anchors, they drifted closer and closer to us. When they were within twenty feet we started to get nervous and stood out on the deck. "Don't worry," they called to us. "We see you—we're moving."

Their boats drifted even closer. "Let's get out of here," Mark said, going to start the engine. By now, there were two drivers in the other boats who at first steered straight for *Mazurka* before correcting the direction. I went up top to man the wheel while Mark began to pull up the anchor. Except it wouldn't come up. The foot pedal on the deck, which started the wheel to pull up the anchor, was always little touchy, but after a good ten minutes it still wasn't working. The other boats had driven safely away, but now we had a new problem: an anchor lodged in the mud at the bottom of Lake Michigan.

Mark got out his tools and an extra foot pedal (it's amazing the assorted gear he had stashed aboard) and commenced to figuring out the problem. I was tired and collected the cats into the bed with me, and the three of us settled down to sleep together.

It was nearly midnight when Mark returned to the cabin. "I figured out the problem!" he proclaimed. "The anchor is powered by the same source as the bow thruster—and I didn't have it on."

If only most equipment problems could be solved this easily.

We decided to stay in the playpen for the night, as the water was calm.

But before the sun was up, I was woken by strong rocking and my husband wide-awake and cleaning up cat puke throughout the cabin. "The wind shifted," he said, wiping his feet. "It's coming out of the northeast. We're going to have rocky waters."

We also had new neighbors, blasting house music at that early-morning hour. They looked like they had been partying all night, as opposed to early-risers up to see the sunrise.

It was not yet six when we pulled up the anchor and began our cruise back to Belmont. The weather report cited ten- to fifteen-mile-an-hour winds from the northeast, rising to fifteen to twenty mph in the afternoon. Instead of cruising up to Milwaukee, we spent the weekend at "Belmont Summer Camp," shooting at the archery range, playing tennis, and running along the lakefront with our *Harbor Dog* neighbors.

Sometimes the best place of all is right outside the front door.

SOCKED IN

Here's a recipe:

Take one powerboat, a thirty-eight-foot Marine Trader trawler, the *Mazurka*.

Give it a captain, Mark, generous, kind, prone to high anxiety.

Add the other liveaboard, the captain's wife, Felicia, a first mate prone to seasickness.

Invite the captain's brother Scott, whom he fights and loves, both to extremes.

Carefully fold in the captain's brother's wife, Jill, who is thirty-two and has breast cancer, has just finished chemo, just had a baby, and is preparing for a mastectomy.

Garnish with the three-month-old baby, Sophia.

Now send them on a four-day fishing trip.

The idea for the trip came about in midsummer, when Jill and Scott had been living in cancer for five months. Jill was diagnosed with breast cancer on Valentine's Day, when she was well into her second trimester of pregnancy. Living in cancer: Yes, it is a place you seem to go, when the rest of the world you have known—jobs and health and freedom to move—is suddenly penned in by a strange mass of vicious cells rapidly growing in your body. Jill had taken a leave from her job, Scott had cut back his hours, and the two of them had submerged themselves in chemo and cancer education and the end of pregnancy and then the birth of beautiful, healthy Sophia, and then taking care of a newborn and finishing chemo, and you can see how several months of this would render someone bleary-eyed and vaguely nauseous, as if they had spent the entire weekend sitting on the couch watching episode after episode of some TV show like *Alias*, or *Six Feet Under*, which is in fact what Jill had been doing, for weeks.

After much discussion, Mark and I decided to invite them aboard *Mazurka* for a fishing trip. They could sleep in the main stateroom, and we would stay in the two bunks up in the bow. Our vague plan—because how much of a definite plan can you make on a boat with a baby?—was to spend the height of summer on the open landscape of Lake Michigan; Mark and Scott would fish for salmon swimming seventy feet below us; Jill and I would play with Sophia in the sun and take her for her first lake swimming lesson; we would clean the day's catch and grill our meal and breeze into a new harbor to spend the night snugly nestled at a dock. It would be a vacation of freedom and wide-open spaces, nothing to stop us from moving ahead with all the comforts of home right around us.

You gotta hand it to Jill and Scott; they were exhausted from cancer treatments, exhausted from having a new baby, yet when the invite came to stay on somebody else's small boat for four days, they said, "Sure."

On the first morning of our fishing trip, we left the harbor just after noon, the sun bright in the cloudless sky as the annual Chicago Air and Water Show sent planes looping and zooming over our heads. We quickly learned that the calm, windless day was an illusion; the lake's rolling waves tossed us back and forth relentlessly. After an hour I claimed the magical wristband to ease my headache and the onset of seasickness. The band's electrical pulses kept the nausea at bay, and I put on my swimsuit and lay out in the sun on the aft cabin. Inside, just beneath me, Jill napped to avoid the nausea. Scott and Mark remained on the flybridge with Sophia, where Mark captained our course. "She's getting a little green," Scott observed of his three month-old daughter, who looked more comfortable than her mother or aunt.

Five hours later, we cruised into calm Waukegan Harbor, grateful for still harbor water. Friendly fellow boaters helped us tie up in the transient slip, and Mark paid for two nights as we set about exploring the harbor, which has terrific amenities: a laundry, spotless shower rooms, free coffee in the office, WiFi, and an ice cream parlor and bait shop nearby.

We grilled dinner and set our places at the dockside covered picnic table. As we said grace, the sky darkened with clouds. We didn't mind a little rain. But by the time we were clearing the plates, the raindrops had grown to dime-sized pellets, and we collected inside just in time to escape the downpour.

In the salon we wrapped in autumn jackets and blankets and watched the wind whip through the sails of a hundred dockside boats. Lightning cracked and we waited for it to hit a neighboring mast. We were safe in the slip, but beyond the breaker wall, we could see the lake swelling with whitecapped waves. The weather radio reported torrential rain and twenty-knot winds. "Maybe we won't be fishing tomorrow after all," Mark said.

Six months earlier, the call came as Mark and I were preparing dinner for our first Valentine's Day as husband and wife. I watched my husband's grim face as he listened to his brother. I knew what he was being told.

Jill's test results had come in, and they were positive.

When Mark passed the phone to me, I sat on the bed, listening to my best friend of twenty years tell me that chemo in the second and third trimesters has surprisingly few side effects on a baby in utero.

"I can't believe we're having this conversation," I said.

"I know."

And then things moved fast. I went to stay with Jill and Scott for the first week of doctor appointments, the time spent making decisions about treatment and a course of action. Chemo, then a mastectomy, then radiation. We spent our days in hospital waiting rooms and restaurants, the only respite a visit to Jill's OB, when the baby's sweet heartbeat filled the exam room, affirming there was life—persistent, hopeful life—amid this unbelievable turn of events.

Action made us feel better—accomplishing things, getting things done, checking them off the list. Jill and I had always been like that, even at twelve years old, going from geography test to band practice to play rehearsal to the movies. We felt best when our lives were in overdrive; it gave us the illusion we were in control.

The opposite—helpless sitting still—had the reverse effect; we felt in control of nothing. Not the weather, not cancer, not what would happen today, tomorrow, or any day. Doing something was only a pacifier.

But a pacifier we needed. For the next two days, while the storm raged outside, we did small things. She knit, I drank coffee. We washed bottles and wiped the counter. We rearranged food in the refrigerator. We ventured outside in hooded jackets, wandering the docks, watching the wind whip the sailboats as if they were toddlers' toys. We read piles of magazines—*The Atlantic, Harper's, Rock and Ice*. We washed load after load of laundry, each of us retreating at some point to the harbor's laundry room for a moment to breathe alone.

In the late afternoons and into the evenings, we played board games. Backgammon, Blokus, Risk. Jill was the only person I'd ever played Risk with—she would cross-stitch or knit, as if not really paying attention, all the while scheming. I had learned not to trust her; she planned her attack slowly, gradually building up, then wiped out opponents in a single blow. I loved playing Risk with Jill and Scott, because I was as competitive as they were. I wanted world domination.

This was Mark's first time playing, so they reviewed the rules. You start with your countries, you get some armies, you fortify. The goal is to take over countries, and then continents, by attacking another player in a game of dice. The more countries and continents you own, the more cards you get, the more armies you amass. The winner is the one who takes over the world.

We had superstitions: Whoever owns Madagascar at the beginning would win. Mark held it in this game.

Jill took Australia. I was planted in Europe. Mark held a lot of Africa. Scott was spread throughout the Americas.

We commenced attacking, dice rolling, trash talking, passing Sophia back and forth so we could defend or attack. Early on, Mark won all of Africa, then struggled to hold it—he looked weak. Scott and Jill discussed who would take him out, thus assuming his countries and the cards he held, which would give them more armies. Bordering him to the north, I was aiming for all of Europe; I told him that I would not attack him. Instead, I went after Jill in Eurasia, and I vocalized my intent to wipe out a path from Europe to Australia, and take that from her, too.

Mark made a crazy attack and took India from Jill.

"That was surprising," Jill and Scott declared.

Suddenly the game shifted, and Jill defended her territories from Mark. Meanwhile, Mark was winning his wars, amassing armies in Africa. He attacked his brother's hold on South America and took it in one sweep. World power shifted. Hours passed, Sophia slept, and Mark, who was the weak one a few hours earlier, now solidly held Africa and South America. Jill was weak in Asia, and I was coming after her, maintaining a strong hold of Europe. Scott struggled to secure North America, trying to convince his wife to help him conquer his brother. She told him, "You only want to take him because he's your nemesis."

It was nearly nine o'clock. We had eaten too much sugar and drunk too much coffee. We were hungry and tired.

"This is a stressful game," Mark observed, "you're constantly being attacked."

We wrapped it up and retired to our bunks.

Lying in twin bunks up in the V-berth, I told Mark how he impressed me with his Risk prowess.

"I wasn't trying to win," he confessed. "I was going to lose anyway. So my strategy was to help you win." He lay back with his hands behind his head. "I wanted to wipe out Jill in Asia to deflect attention from you."

My admiration and appreciation swelled for the captain.

Who plays Risk, not for their own personal gain, but for their opponent's? Yet by trying to help me, he changed the dynamic of the game, and ended up taking two continents and becoming a major player.

I like the captain's philosophy in life: When it's clear you're going to lose, may as well help somebody else on your way out.

On the eve of the second full day of rain, when the storm showed no sign of respite, we began to feel like Bradbury characters in a world without sun. We stopped waiting for the one day of sunshine and discussed the possibility of leaving in the storm. We debated the time-versus-discomfort ratio, and the maximum tolerable height for waves (five feet? ten?). *Mazurka* was worthy of a storm, but every single item inside—our entire home—would be dislodged and thrown in a matter of minutes. Not to mention the seasickness. There was also the possibility that even if the rain subsided, the lake could remain tumultuous for another day.

Mark and Scott told stories of the *Isle Royale Queen*, the passenger boat between the UP and Isle Royale. Lake Superior natives nicknamed it "the Barf Bucket."

"They added on to the top of it, so its sits really high in the water and rolls like a son of a bitch."

"Sometimes after a really bad trip, it glistens."

"What, from rain?" we asked.

"No—from vomit."

We made contingency plans. The suburban commuter train stopped right outside the harbor, and if necessary Jill and Scott and Sophia could take the train into Chicago, then a cab to Belmont Harbor where their car waited. But our house would stay socked in at Waukegan Harbor. If nothing else, Mark and I could become temporary suburbanites, taking the commuter train into work on Tuesday morning, and returning at night to our new suburban home.

Early Monday morning, my dreamy sleep was pierced by Mark telling Jill, "Better check the train schedules."

The captain came in to tell me, "We have a new problem."

Outside, the sky was a pale, oyster-colored overcast, but lacking rain clouds; the lake was calm. The problem—which Mark discovered when preparing to start the engine—turned out to be diesel fuel in the oil. This was much worse than any temporary storm.

Mark and Scott debated about whether or not to start the engine. There was a small window of opportunity; the lake was serene, but storms were predicted for the afternoon. Scott wanted to take the chance, but Mark, as captain, made the final decision. He called a cab to pick him up on an errand for new oil and filters.

While Scott and I pumped the bad oil by hand into a bucket, I asked him what I often wondered at times like these—if owning a house was like owning a boat, in terms of repairs and upkeep. "Well, in a house things are never done," he began, "but you don't have an engine, you don't have so many mechanics. So a boat is worse." Which was what I was coming to accept, despite my captain's assurances that we would always have problems, no matter where we lived.

Above us, Jill sat at the table amid stacks of reading material and baby gear, the floor of the salon open to us in the engine room below.

"How do you like the chaos?" I asked, looking up at her.

"I always hear about it, and now I get to see it firsthand," she said, smiling.

When Mark returned, he changed the oil, and the engine started up right away.

Bracing ourselves for the ride home, we found the lake to be calm, innocent, as if she were never capable of ten-foot waves and who were we to think she could possibly be so tumultuous? Just a few miles from shore, we could barely make out the landmarks as we headed south, except for the Bahai Temple, rising from the mist like a lacy ethereal rocket.

We came through four days of twenty- to thirty-knot winds, thunder and lightning, crashing waves and heavy rain—and found the worst of it to be our anticipation.

It was the vacation where no one got what they wanted: We didn't fish, we didn't swim, we didn't cruise off into the wild blue yonder. We sat trapped, in a boat, for four days. At any moment, one of us could have decided enough's enough and pushed somebody's buttons, just to relieve the pressure of standing still, of not knowing the future.

We could have forced a solution. We could have panicked and made our way back through the storm, enduring a hell ride that would have rendered us all sick and our house a disaster. We could have taken a chance and started the engine with fuel in the oil. Instead, we bided our time. We endured sitting. Sometimes, sitting still isn't just the only thing to do; sometimes, it's the right thing to do. The next right action can simply be breathing through it—and helping others to breathe through it, too.

The rain resumed just as we cruised into Belmont Harbor. We tied up in our home slip, found diesel in the oil again, and then suddenly the water heater started to leak. So now we had two problems.

But in a year of living aboard, I had learned there were always problems on a boat. It was not unusual to wake up in the morning and find the floor of the salon missing and my husband in his underwear with a manual and a bunch of tools and a befuddled expression. There was often something going wrong, and usually more than one thing at once—and none of it was worth getting worked up over. That's just life on a boat.

(The small things made me grateful. With the six-gallon water heater on the fritz, we could buy a new one—a bigger one. Yes indeed, folks, our new water heater held ten and a half gallons!)

CRUISING THE THIRD COAST

There are two kinds of vacations: the one where you go away, and the one where you stay home. Going away, you can explore new places, meet new people, do new things. Staying home, you can relax in your own home and catch up on all the projects you've been meaning to get to.

Mark and I combined the two in an eight-day trip up the "Third Coast," also known as "Wisconsin."

We had successfully navigated our second year of marriage aboard *Mazurka*. The winter had been relatively calm (though the pumpout froze again). We were back in Belmont Harbor for the summer, this time on G Dock. We had grown used to the challenges of boat life. We wondered if the novelty was wearing thin.

Every harbor we planned to visit during our vacation was within a two-and-a-half-hour car ride from Chicago, but aboard *Mazurka*, our destinations would seem exotic and faraway.

In a sea of fog, we left Belmont Harbor for northern ports.

Granted, Waukegan Harbor is only thirty-eight nautical miles north. Driving, it would take about an hour, even with construction. Aboard *Mazurka*, it took four hours.

While you might not think of Waukegan as a weekend getaway destination, the home of Ray Bradbury and Jack Benny has a beautiful harbor and hands down the best Fourth of July fireworks show anywhere. Chicagoans should forget the crowds at Navy Pier and haul themselves up to Waukegan where a symphony plays in the harbor, followed by a forty-five-minute fireworks show that explodes right overhead (watch for falling cinders). If you spend the night, make sure to head downtown for brunch at Hussey's, a biker bar with terrific biscuits and gravy and homemade sausage.

After an overnight stay in Waukegan, we cruised over glass-like water for our next port, Racine.

I had driven past Racine hundreds of times. Not once had I ever stopped to explore it. Too bad, because it's a beautiful town. French missionaries who came in the nineteenth century found a natural harbor created by the tangle of tree roots along the shore where the Root River meets Lake Michigan and named the town Racine, French for "root." For most of the twentieth century, the shoreline was industrial, until the late 1980s when the area was rebuilt into a harbor complex.

After a morning spent in search of alternator belts and washing seven loads of laundry in the harbor Laundromat, the sky cleared to a beautiful blue and we hopped on our bikes for a tour of the town via the Root River Pathway, which connected with the numerous bike routes of southeast Wisconsin. We followed signs through neighborhood streets, a gravel path through Colonial Park, and paved riverside roads.

The next morning, as we prepared to leave Racine for Port Washington, a six-hour cruise, there were clear blue skies and a marine forecast of winds out of the Northeast, ten to fifteen knots, waves two to four feet.

"It's going to be rocky," Mark warned.

Not that I didn't believe him; I just had this idea that we would be granted special clearance. Like God would split the waves just to make a calm path for our six-hour journey. I fully expected to be in the City of Seven Hills by dinner.

Those two- to four-foot waves were closer to five or six. Luckily we were heading into the waves, rather than rolling sideways, so that our nose went up and down. At the helm, I concentrated on keeping my muscles loose, hands and jaw unclenched; tension only makes seasickness worse.

While I managed the roller-coaster ride at the helm, Mark checked the engine room. Gray clouds rolled in from the west, so that half the lake was blue beneath clear skies, the other half gray and stormy. Milwaukee loomed in the distance. We kept riding the waves, spray shooting over the bow of the boat, soaking us up on the flybridge. The field of whitecaps in front of us grew larger; with three more hours to Port Washington, we made a detour into Milwaukee. Mark took the helm and I made sure nothing fell overboard as we tilted back and forth at twenty-degree angles. As we headed toward shore, rocking side-to-side, I fleetingly thought of the chaos happening in-side the cabin, and our poor cats. But at this point, it was every man for himself.

Once docked at McKinley Marina, we went down into the cabin. The place had been ransacked by reckless thieves. The stereo and lamp lay on their sides, the kitchen counter on the floor, the contents of the fridge across the room. There were books and papers and draw-ers all over the forward cabin. I hadn't tightened the windows in the forward cabin, and the entire office—including computers—was wet. Hunter and Leo were huddled, terrified, near our pillows in the aft cabin, cat puke everywhere.

I was mad. Mad at myself for not battening down the hatches, mad that electronics were wet, mad that the cats were sick, and mad we were in Milwaukee. Milwaukee is a fine city—but it's just that: a city. McKinley Marina and its encompassing park looked far too much like our home in Belmont Harbor. The sound of traffic and sirens in the distance was daily life, and this was vacation. I wanted quaint, provincial towns. But at least we were safe, and nothing was broken, and even though it was a pain to put everything back in its rightful place, in a couple of hours we were done.

We spent a low-key evening in the City of Clocks. I caught up on emails and phone calls, Mark fixed stuff: the cup holder on the flybridge and a wind chime; he even got out his sewing machine and stitched up torn pants. I kept turning on the weather report, hoping it would suddenly change, but it remained constant: The forecast for Wednesday was northeast winds of ten to fifteen knots, waves two to four feet. Exactly what we'd just come through.

"The boat can handle it," Mark said, "but can we?"

Before going to bed, I made myself stand out on the deck and take in the city. I was powerless over the weather. If we had to spend another day in Milwaukee, we could visit the art museum and the farmers market and bike around. Maybe it wasn't what I was expecting, but it would be okay.

The next morning, Mark was up early, returning from Home Depot with a new bolt for the alternator and some coffee for me before it was even seven o'clock. "It looks calm out there," he said. "Let's make a run for it."

We battened down the hatches for real this time, preparing for the worst. And though the weather report was exactly the same, the lake was completely different—she was calm, soothing, without a white-cap in sight.

I learned something important that day: Weather reports and radars are not to be relied upon. Better to look at the reality right in front of you. And listen to the captain when he says, "Let's make a run for it!"

"A combination of New England charm and Midwestern friend-liness," the tourism site for Port Washington proclaims—and it's no marketing scam. The City of Seven Hills has friendly people and a beautiful lakefront. You might not even notice the huge generating station looming to the south. (But if you do, take heart: What was the world's most efficient coal-fired plant in 1935 has been rebuilt into a cleaner, more efficient gas-fired power plant.)

At noon we arrived in "The Port" as locals call it, docked *Mazurka* in a transient slip, and strolled downtown. The ladies at the visitors

center heaped menus and maps on us. We ate a Mexican meal at
Beanie's, bought lilies and rare blue orchids at Brown's, found Polish
sausage and Wisconsin cheese at Bernie's and pants and shirts for
Mark at Anchor Men's Store, where the attentive, friendly, not-too-
pushy salesman happily offered to tailor Mark's cuffs.

As we wandered back to the boat, I got an eerie feeling. "This place
is too perfect," I told Mark. "It's like some episode of *Twilight Zone*—
young couple visits small midwestern town, never seen again."

But a good place to look for us would be the miles and miles of
paved bike paths linking these small towns and the lakefront. We
spent two more days cycling the crushed-limestone trails and back-
country highways.

The harbor in Port Washington was packed with charter fishing
boats. We were given a slip between two of them. They left early in
the morning—around 4 a.m.—which on our first morning had me

believing in my dream-state that Mark was going to make me get up and go out with them.

Midmorning I was out on deck when I noticed a trend in the people wandering the harbor walk: groups of moms, grandmas, little kids. When a charter boat came in, all the groups would approach the boat; one group would remain, the other groups would wander off to continue waiting. I realized I was watching an ancient ritual: women waiting for their fishermen to come in.

On our second morning, one of our neighbors, *Fishing Pox*, returned around eight o'clock. I reasoned the fishing must have been fantastic and they caught their limit early. We came out to see their catch. Surprisingly, the boat held just the captain, his wife, and some of their friends. They had gone out for fun.

One of the friends prepared to clean their catch on the dock. He opened the cooler to reveal three pan-sized fish (two king salmon and one rainbow trout), and one large mother of a king, maybe three feet long, its back glistening pink, its tail spotted black, and one eye watching us.

"Who caught that one?" I asked.

"The captain," his friend said.

Gus, the captain, was the only charter fisherman in Port Washington who went out fishing on his morning off. "When it stops being fun," he told me, "I'll quit doing it."

We can love something so much we decide to take it as a career. If it's really a vocation, we'll do it on our day off. There's always the mother king waiting to be caught.

When traveling by boat, it's wise to leave an extra day at the end in case bad weather prevents you from cruising home in time for work Monday morning. Wouldn't want to miss that.

Or, as in our case, the extra day can be used when you come into an unexpectedly fun harbor.

Kenosha was an afterthought; we knew we'd need a stop between Port Washington and Belmont, and we'd already explored Racine and Waukegan, so Kenosha seemed the logical choice for something "fresh," as Mark put it. As in, "I like vacations where we do something fresh and creative."

(This statement cracked me up. Is living on a boat "fresh"? I guess you could call it that.)

On our last night in Port Washington, we serendipitously met some Kenosha harbor citizens who gave us the lowdown on the ever-expanding harbor.

When we arrived in Kenosha the following afternoon, half a dozen fellow boaters greeted us on the dock, helping us to maneuver into the narrow slip and tie up. They spotted the bikes on the aft deck and asked if we had come for the international bike race, "Food, Folks and Spokes."

As we experienced in every other harbor, trawlers are like goodwill ambassadors of the boating world. Sailors and powerboaters alike are attracted. "You can tell this is a loved boat," one sailor told us.

We spent the extra day in Kenosha cycling the county bike trail back north to Racine, to the lighthouse on the northern end of town. We left just after noon, stopped for a leisurely two-hour lunch at Ivanhoe in downtown Racine, biked the rest of the way to the lighthouse, and got back to our dock in Kenosha around six thirty.

Total biking miles for the week: seventy.

Total boating miles for the week: 190.

Total ice creams eaten: Who's counting?

Sunday morning, we left Kenosha under overcast skies and a slight western wind. Just north of Waukegan, we encountered a large barge off the starboard and suddenly found ourselves surrounded by fishing boats, fanning out to the horizon. Mark sat to my left, reading, as I manned the helm, steering clear of everyone. There was something eerie about passing through so many silent, still boats in the early light, like a graveyard of ghost ships. I felt we had to be very quiet to not disturb any of them out of respect. It reminded me of the ancient mariners, Greek and Norse, and the mythology that evolved on the water when sailors spent days upon days out at sea, listening with their eyes to the sky and the waves, tasting the wind with their skin.

Something different happens to us on the water. Something indescribable, though we keep trying to find words for it. Something about so much space and so much hidden depth that opens the mind and the imagination. A limitless expanse of nothingness, full of possibility, ready for exploration.

I finally accepted there were three of us in this marriage—Mark, me, and *Mazurka*. In the beginning, flung around a can in Monroe Harbor, or stuck in the ice on the Chicago River, I resented the hell out of this fact. But after nearly two years of marriage, if *Mazurka* needed it, I would have carried her over land like an Argonaut.

Maybe we come to love something most when we realize we may have to give it up.

GHOSTS IN WHITE PLASTIC

We had been married and living aboard *Mazurka* for two years when Mark was offered his dream job—in Duluth, Minnesota.

We were sitting in the Red Apple, a Polish buffet on North Milwaukee Avenue, on a rainy September evening when Mark announced over pierogi and potato pancakes, "I'm ready to rejoin the world."

He talked about the world of isolation he created by living on the

water. "I don't even pay property taxes," he said. "How do you rejoin society?"

I considered our possible transition back to land—it had been two years on water for me, four years for Mark—and where we might live in northern Minnesota. I wondered if that was any more a part of society than living aboard a boat in downtown Chicago.

"What if you never really left society?" I asked.

"You mean it was just an illusion?"

"Yeah," I said. "In a way, you expanded society. Think of all the people you brought on board and showed a different view of Chicago. They would never have seen the city that way if it hadn't been for you."

For Mark, living on the boat was a way to detach from the world, to avoid the ties that bind one to the land of the ordinary everyday. Want to escape for a bit? Pull up anchor and head out to deeper water.

For me, living on *Mazurka* was my commitment to Mark. And in the two years we spent together on board, I learned how to be his wife. I learned how to willingly, with *joy* even, take that pumpout hose and hook it up to the sewage outlet and watch gallons of waste run through. In the second year, when the sewage overflowed into the bilge, I climbed down into the bilge with the pumpout hose and sucked up the overflow. I learned how to get past the "Well, this is *his* boat" mentality and take responsibility for my part in things. I learned how to compromise, how to give in when I didn't want to go out, how to do my share in a project I never wanted in the first place. It was Mark I wanted, and I owed it to him to show up and do the work assigned. Living on *Mazurka*, living the transient lifestyle of a liveaboard—surprise surprise—taught me commitment.

"It's going to be hard for him to sell his boat," my mom advised me over the phone. She had married a fisherman; she knew what she was talking about. And I was past the age where I knew too much to listen to her. I felt something stirring in me, something grave, and knew it would be my job to help him through it.

A new topic of conversation swam between us: to sell or not to sell. Though Mark talked about possibly selling *Mazurka*, he wasn't set on it. Duluth sits right on the western corner of Lake Superior. Wasn't there some amazing cruising to be done up there? Sure, with temperatures plunging to negative thirty in the winter, it would be a long shot to even find a harbor willing to host year-round liveaboards. But what about keeping the boat for recreation? A floating cabin. Four hours from Duluth stood the Apostle Islands—what Mark liked to call "the Bahamas of the North." And farther out, there was magnificent Isle Royale. And what about the trip to get her up to Duluth? Mark was giddy at the possibilities. Maybe this was just the next leg of our adventure together, more ports to explore.

We decided to keep her, for now. We would stay in Belmont Harbor until November 15. Then we would take *Mazurka* down the river to a winter storage unit, where she would stay until the following spring. We weren't leaving Chicago until mid-December, but that was too late to hoist her out of the water. Instead, we would spend our final month in Chicago on land—or rather, in the air—in a thirteenth-floor rented furnished condo. After moving to Duluth in December, we would wait until spring to figure out how to get *Mazurka* up north.

One morning in our last month on *Mazurka*, in the few weeks before leaving Belmont Harbor, Mark went out the door for work and I stood in the doorway, waving to him as he carried his briefcase and blue lunch bag with the sandwich I had just made him. He turned on the dock to look back at the boat. I opened the door to see if he needed something. He stood looking at the side of the hull, then at me, his eyes taking in the whole scene. It occurred to me that he wasn't looking at anything in particular—he was taking it all in, as an impressionist painter does. He was checking the condition of his boat, as he often did, and as he did, he was checking the condition of his life. This was his life: boat, wife, water.

Time to pull up anchor and head to a different harbor. This life was coming to a close. We would soon be bound for land, for the unknown.

I was grateful to be spending our last days aboard *Mazurka* in Belmont Harbor, where we watched the autumnal sunrise over the lake in the morning, curtained by the orange and yellow leaves of our luxurious backyard. A city park that felt so intimate, as if it belonged only to us. In the evenings, we sat in the salon and watched the sparkling view of downtown, the Hancock building now almost overshadowed by Trump's new tower, and the water all around us reflecting lamplight from the rows and rows of condos lining Lake Michigan, as real as van Gogh's *Starry Night*.

True to the end, our final days as liveaboards weren't without the unexpected challenges. Although Belmont Harbor was supposed to keep its water on until November 15, they decided to turn it off early. Maybe because temperatures plunged below freezing; who was I to judge? In our few last days aboard, we resorted to some creative ways of filling the water tanks. (Picture Mark on the dock holding plastic five-gallon jugs strung up like a bouquet of balloons he's peddling.)

On Saturday night, after Mark and I had spent all day shuttling boxes from *Mazurka* to storage, I asked him, "Do you think someday we might look back on this and think we were crazy for living on a boat?"

"Someday might be tomorrow," he replied.

Sunday morning we found a brief lull in the gale-force winds and took *Mazurka* down the Chicago River. After being hauled out, she sat comfortably in a cradle in heated storage, beside million-dollar yachts.

I took one final picture of her in the water. *Till we meet again,* I thought, because I felt melancholy and dramatic. In reality, till we meet again turned out to be the next weekend, when we returned to give her a good thorough scrubbing.

Walking among boats in heated storage was like swimming underwater with ghosts. They were hoisted up high, so that we walked beneath the waterline, their plastic covers rustling softly around us.

The first thing Mark and I noticed when we climbed (and I mean climbed) aboard *Mazurka* was that she felt like she should be moving, even though she wasn't.

It was a strange, lonesome feeling.

We spent Saturday afternoon doing the last cleaning of the season, but for different reasons. Mark was cleaning in case a potential buyer needed to come aboard. (He was still considering selling her, despite our daily discussion ending in, "Okay, we'll keep her for now.") I was cleaning so that she would be fresh and ready when we took her up north the next summer.

I was having a hard time leaving her.

Mark, surprisingly, was ready for the next adventure.

"I got tired of the transient lifestyle," he confessed. "The pumpouts not working, the electricity going out, and then when they shut off our water in Belmont Harbor, that was it."

I had learned to accept all that inconvenience as boat life. In exchange, I got the sky and the water constantly beneath me. Not a week off *Mazurka*, I missed the water. Sure, we could see the lake and the sky from our fancy furnished South Loop condo. It wasn't the same. We were always the same temperature; we were always level.

At night, I still felt the water beneath me.

I dreamed of diving off the back platform and swimming the Chicago River in the big-shouldered shadow of the Merchandise Mart and the Sears Tower. Lengthening my stroke, swimming back and forth along the tree-lined riverfront, I wondered in the dream why I never swam the river in the two years I lived on *Mazurka*. I felt this terrible longing and regret for all the things I would never be able to do now that we were leaving.

When I woke, full of remorse, I remembered the Chicago River was still not fit for swimming. But maybe someday, for some live-aboard newlyweds, it will be translucent and clean, and they can dive right in.

IRON MAN

His name is Rafael. We shortened it to Rafe. His grandmother calls him Rafey. When he started to say his own name, he pronounced it "Fe." So that's what we call him. Fe. We joke about it being the elemental symbol for iron, that he is Iron Man.

It was a warm September Sunday when we took Fe and his baby sister, Esther—who was just a month old—out to the boat. When it was just the two of us, we lived on *Mazurka* year-round in downtown Chicago. Now there are four of us, and we live on land in northern Minnesota, and every weekend we trek up to Knife River and our floating cabin on Lake Superior.

On this particular Sunday, we planned to swing by the boat to check a few things, then go for a hike.

We had just gotten to *Mazurka*. Mark was inside the cabin, Fe was with him. I was at the car securing our month-old daughter to my chest in a newfangled wrap. As I walked out to the dock, Fe was just starting to climb out of the boat, onto the stepladder. I stood behind him and watched him descend, carefully, as a two-year-old does. His feet crossed, and I watched him straighten them out, watched as he figured out how to correct the cross. There was a brief moment where I saw myself watching him, watching my two-year-old climb out of the boat, and wasn't I wise for letting him untangle his feet on his own? For not rushing to help him at the slightest misstep?

It was the bottom step he missed. His feet were not crossed; I don't know what happened. But as I watched, he slipped to the dock, lay on his back for a second, then rolled over into the water between the dock and *Mazurka*.

He was not wearing a life jacket.

I have spent more than a few days flogging myself for not putting him in a life jacket that afternoon. It was the rule that he wore one. But we were only going to be there a minute.

Then it all happened so fast. On my day of reckoning I will get to watch the recap and then I'll know what really happened. But today, what I recall is that I got down on my knees and, with Esther strapped to my chest, tried to reach for him. I grabbed hold of his sweatshirt, something so flimsy it just slipped through my fingers. He went under. I screamed for Mark, then climbed down into the water. Maybe I fell. I think I must have climbed, because I kept one hand on the dock four feet above the water's surface, while keeping Esther's head above water as she stayed tight to my chest. I wanted to grab him with my free hand, but when I reached out, he was gone.

In my mind's eye I imagined my son in eight feet of murky green Lake Superior water, sinking to the bottom.

Mark came out, calling, "Where is he?"

"I don't see him," I yelled. Mark jumped in the water on the other side of the dock. Why he didn't jump in right where Fe fell in, we don't know.

Then, through the space between floats under the dock, I could see Fe, treading water. He was inches from his dad.

I yelled out, "I see him," and I heard Mark saying, "I got you, I got you." I felt a rush of relief; he was safe. There was splashing and flailing, and I wondered if Mark really had him and could get him onto land.

In the small gap between the boat and the dock, *Mazurka* began to close in on me. I pushed my back against it; I had to figure out a way to get us out of the water. My four-week-old daughter wouldn't do well in lake water for too long. I wasn't sure what to grab, or what to climb. I noticed Mark making his way along the side of the dock, toward the stern of the boat, where the swim platform and extendable ladder waited. I followed, keeping Esther's head above water. Remarkably, she wasn't crying, just looking around.

At the platform, Mark had Fe on the ladder, telling him to climb up. Fe was crying, but following directions. Then Mark climbed up and put our son safely on the deck of the boat. I was still in the water with Esther, and couldn't get ahold of the ladder well enough to leverage us out, so Mark reached down, and I raised our tiny wet newborn up to him. I climbed the ladder. We hurried inside the cabin, stripped everybody naked, and huddled together under sleeping bags to warm our kids.

The funny thing was, the water wasn't even that cold.

How does a two-year-old fall into Lake Superior and make his way under a six-foot-wide dock to where his dad randomly chooses to jump in to find him?

We questioned Fe to find out what exactly had happened. He wasn't talking. At first we thought the whole experience had permanently scarred him, that he'd be mute for life. Then he asked to go up to the salon to play, then for snacks. He showed us how he dog-paddled; he didn't seem scared at all.

Fe doesn't swim. He's two years old, and he doesn't like cold water. A couple of months earlier we took him to a water park and he dog-paddled in the hot tub while wearing a life jacket. We cruised for ten days in the Apostles just before Esther was born, and while Mark and

I swam in warm Lake Superior water, Fe stayed on the beaches, proclaiming the water too cold. How he managed to swim under the dock, to the exact spot where Mark jumped in, only to be plucked up by his dad instantly . . . we don't know.

While I was in the water, all I could think was that he was sinking. This is what people do—they fall in, panic, sink. This is how people drown. When I didn't see him, I was sure he was going down. In that brief thirty-second window, all I could think was that he was going to die. That the most important person in my life would be gone in a second, and it would be my fault for not saving him.

In the hours and days and now months since the event happened, I am still trying to sort it out. Fe has heard us tell the story so many times that he tells it, too, taking on the role of the narrator and referring to us by our first names. I am convinced that we witnessed a miracle. But receiving a miracle does not bring breathless gratitude the way I once thought it would. Instead, I oscillate between guilt that I failed my son, guilt that I do not deserve this miracle, and awe that something like this could happen. We stood at a crossroads that day, and in another world we lost our son to the bottom of a harbor; but in this world, some unseen hand reached down and taught the Iron Man to swim.

CODA

For two seasons *Mazurka* has sat idly in her cradles. On land.

We've been adjusting to life on land, too. We bought a tent and a snowblower. Our house is filled with toys and Strider bikes. Things have definitely changed.

Some things are the same. My last drink happened that Father's Day weekend aboard *Mazurka*. Today, my life sober is more abundant than anything I could have imagined while I was still drinking.

And *Mazurka* still resonates quietly, a current at the heart of our marriage. A portrait of her sits over our fireplace, reminding us every day that she carried us at the start of our married life.

This summer Rafe will be five—a little more responsible, sure-footed, and helpful (not to mention maneuverable) in the engine room. Esther will be three. She's less squirrelly than Rafe was at that age. Our baby Anton won't be walking yet. Can we manage three kids on *Mazurka*? If they live in their life jackets, if we have plans in place for emergencies, if we take it slowly, setting up boundaries and precautions and teaching our kids how to conduct themselves on a boat—can we do it?

If we *don't* do it now, then when?

Now we have the chance to give our kids the joy of tossing the lines and pushing offshore, away from land, free. They get to learn how to care for a boat, how to balance periods of intense work with the slow pace of being under way. And how to live together, peaceably, in a small space with only the essentials.*

It will be a lot different with two kids in the V-berth, and a Pack 'n Play for the baby taking up the salon.

I think we're up for the challenge.

All five of us atop the lighthouse on Michigan Island, in the Apostle Islands National Lakeshore, July 2015. Between us, *Mazurka* peeks out from where she is anchored just offshore.

*Essentials: Water, food, map, books, towel. Engine oil. Flashlights. Batteries. Boat hooks. Net. Some glue for when the Zodiac pops a hole. Fly swatter. Cell phone. Laptop. Four seasons of clothing 'cause you never know what the weather is like on the Big Lake. Bag of toys. Pack 'n Play. Another bag of toys. More books. Snacks. Lots of snacks. Diapers. Piles of diapers. You don't want to have to make a diaper run in some godforsaken harbor, especially a harbor with ice cream stands and playgrounds.